PART 2

Rex Jones II, CSTE, TMap

You Must Learn
VBScript
for QTP/UFT

Don't Ignore
The Language
For Functional
Automation Testing

Free Webinars, Videos, and Live Training

Mr. Jones plans to have **free** step-by-step demonstration webinars, videos, and live trainings walking people through concepts of QTP/UFT and Selenium from A - Z. The material will teach/train individuals the fundamentals of the programming language, fundamentals of QTP/UFT and Selenium, and important concepts of QTP/UFT and Selenium. All of the webinars, videos, and live training will be directed toward beginners as well as mid-level automation engineers.

Sign Up to Receive

1. 3 Tips To Master QTP/UFT Within 30 Days
   http://tinyurl.com/3-Tips-For-QTP-UFT

2. 3 Tips To Master Selenium Within 30 Days
   http://tinyurl.com/3-Tips-For-Selenium

3. Free Webinars, Videos, and Live Trainings
   http://tinyurl.com/Free-QTP-UFT-Selenium

Skype: rex.jones34
Twitter: @RexJonesII
Email: Rex.Jones@Test4Success.org
LinkedIn: https://www.linkedin.com/in/rexjones34

Preface

Part 2 – You Must Learn VBScript for QTP/UFT is a reference book for automation engineers. Automation engineers will need to understand the basics of VBScript to benefit from the contents of this book. VBScript enables automation engineers to accomplish many tasks and each task assists QTP/UFT with testing any Application Under Test (AUT).

Target Audience

The target audience is automation engineers with a solid foundation of VBScript. Automation engineers who occupy an understanding of variables, data types, operators, arrays, flow control, functions, and how to create/destroy objects. It is recommended to read Part 1 – You Must Learn VBScript for QTP/UFT, if an individual needs to gain a foundation in VBScript.

Purpose

The purpose of this book is to provide automation engineers with a deeper knowledge of VBScript. VBScript is a lightweight programming language that possesses powerful features. Features such as objects and regular expressions help VBScript emulate programming languages like Visual Basic. Learning some of the powerful features of VBScript facilitates several tasks to be created with less lines of code.

3 Tips To Master QTP/UFT Within 30 Days
http://tinyurl.com/3-Tips-For-QTP-UFT

Free Webinars, Videos, and Live Trainings
http://tinyurl.com/Free-QTP-UFT-Selenium

About the Author

Rex Allen Jones II is a QA/Software Tester with a passion for sharing knowledge about testing software. He has been watching webinars, attending seminars, and testing applications since February 2005. Mr. Jones graduated from DeVry University in June 1999 with a Bachelor's of Science degree in Computer Information Systems (CIS).

Currently, Rex is a Sr. Consultant and former Board of Director for User Group: Dallas / Fort Worth Mercury User Group (DFWMUG) and member of User Group: Dallas / Fort Worth Quality Assurance Association (DFWQAA). In addition to his User Group memberships, he is a Certified Software Tester Engineer (CSTE) and has a Test Management Approach (TMap) certification.

Mr. Jones' advice for people interested in Functional Automation Testing is to learn the programming language. This advice led him to write 4 programming books "(Part 1 & Part 2)

Skype: rex.jones34
Twitter: @RexJonesII
Email: Rex.Jones@Test4Success.org
LinkedIn: https://www.linkedin.com/in/rexjones34

You Must Learn VBScript for QTP/UFT" and "(Part 1 & Part 2) Java 4 Selenium WebDriver". VBScript is the programming language for Unified Functional Testing (UFT) formerly known as Quick Test Professional (QTP) and Java is one of the programming languages for Selenium WebDriver.

3 Tips To Master QTP/UFT Within 30 Days
http://tinyurl.com/3-Tips-For-QTP-UFT

Free Webinars, Videos, and Live Trainings
http://tinyurl.com/Free-QTP-UFT-Selenium

About the Editor

When Samantha Mann is not improving the contents of a document through constructive editing marks and remarks, she is enjoying life as a professional in Dallas, Texas. Samantha is a User Experience guru in the realms of research and design, and works as an Information Technology consultant. Outside of work her hobbies include the typical nerd-type fun of freelance editing, reading, writing, and binge watching Netflix with her pitbull.

Connect with Samantha:

Samantha.danae.mann@gmail.com

https://www.linkedin.com/pub/samantha-mann/84/9b7/100

Skype: rex.jones34
Twitter: @RexJonesII
Email: Rex.Jones@Test4Success.org
LinkedIn: https://www.linkedin.com/in/rexjones34

Copyright, Legal Notice, and Disclaimer

3 Tips To Master QTP/UFT Within 30 Days
http://tinyurl.com/3-Tips-For-QTP-UFT

Free Webinars, Videos, and Live Trainings
http://tinyurl.com/Free-QTP-UFT-Selenium

Acknowledgements

I would like to express my gratitude to my wife Tiffany, children Olivia Rexe' and Rex III, editor Samantha Mann, family, friends, and the many people who provided encouragement. Writing this book took time and your support helped pushed this book forward.

Thank You,

Rex Allen Jones II

Skype: rex.jones34
Twitter: @RexJonesII
Email: Rex.Jones@Test4Success.org
LinkedIn: https://www.linkedin.com/in/rexjones34

Chapter 1
Introduction

Overview

There are many programming languages in the Information Technology (IT) industry. This multitude of languages makes a decision to learn a programming language overwhelming and difficult. However, QTP/UFT utilizes VBScript—a powerful scripting language. The first book "(Free) Part 1—You Must Learn VBScript for QTP/UFT" sets the groundwork for this book "Part 2—You Must Learn VBScript for QTP/UFT."

Part 1 explained Variables and Data Types, Operators, Arrays, Flow Control, Procedures – Functions, and how to Create and Destroy Objects. The final chapter "Create and Destroy Objects" is an introduction for Part 2 chapters regarding "Dictionary Objects, FileSystemObject (FSO), and Classes."

This chapter provides an overview rather than details on the following topics by focusing on VBScript's general concepts:

- ✓ Dictionary Objects
- ✓ FileSystemObject (FSO)
- ✓ Classes
- ✓ Regular Expressions
- ✓ Debugging and Handling Errors
- ✓ Windows Script Host (WSH)
- ✓ Windows Management Instrumentation (WMI)

3 Tips To Master QTP/UFT Within 30 Days
http://tinyurl.com/3-Tips-For-QTP-UFT

Free Webinars, Videos, and Live Trainings
http://tinyurl.com/Free-QTP-UFT-Selenium

Dictionary Objects

Dictionary objects are objects that store key/item pairs *(see Dictionary Objects in Chapter 2.)* The keys can be integers or strings while the items can be integers, strings, or arrays. Dictionary objects contains the following methods and properties:

Figure 1.1 – Dictionary Objects Methods and Properties

Methods	Properties
Add	Count
Exists	Item
Items	Key
Keys	CompareMode
Remove	
Remove All	

FileSystemObject (FSO)

FileSystemObject (FSO) accesses a computer's file system via Drives, Folders, and Files *(see FileSystemObject (FSO) in Chapter 3.)* The Drive object provides information about drives connected to the system. All of the file properties are accessed by the File object. The Folder object provides a way to manipulate all of the folder properties. FileSystemObject (FSO) consists of FSO Objects, FSO Collections, Methods, and Properties.

Classes

Classes are templates for objects *(see Classes in Chapter 4.)* The following are covered in Classes:

- o   Class Properties – stores data in an object or returns data from the object

Skype: rex.jones34
Twitter: @RexJonesII
Email: Rex.Jones@Test4Success.org
LinkedIn: https://www.linkedin.com/in/rexjones34

o   Class Methods – operates like a procedure (Sub or Function)

o   Class Events – consist of two events Class Initialize and Class Terminate.) Class Initialize calls a specific class when an object is instantiated while Class Terminate destroys the object

Regular Expressions

Regular expressions are used for locating and/or replacing patterns *(see Regular Expressions in Chapter 5.)* A pattern is a combination of numbers, characters, and/or special characters forming a string. The RegExp object is a built-in object which makes regular expressions available for automation engineers. There are three RegExp object properties and three methods:

Figure 1.2 – RegExp Properties and Methods

Properties	Methods
Global	Execute
IgnoreCase	Replace
Pattern	Test

Debugging and Handling Errors

Debugging is the process of locating and correcting errors, while error-handling is the anticipation, detection, and then resolution of errors in the code. *(see Debugging and Handling Errors in Chapter 6.)* There are three types of errors along with two elements for handling errors:

Error Types

3 Tips To Master QTP/UFT Within 30 Days
http://tinyurl.com/3-Tips-For-QTP-UFT

Free Webinars, Videos, and Live Trainings
http://tinyurl.com/Free-QTP-UFT-Selenium

1. <u>Syntax</u> – error that stop the execution of a program
2. <u>Runtime</u> – occurs when a program executes an invalid action
3. <u>Logical</u> – errors from an automation engineer's programming code logic

Error-Handling Elements

1. <u>Err Object</u> –contains information about a runtime error
2. <u>On Error Statement</u> – regulates the error control settings

Windows Script Host (WSH)

Windows Script Host (WSH) is a Windows administration tool (automation technology) which creates an environment for hosting scripts *(see <u>Windows Script Host (WSH) in Chapter 7</u>.)* There are two interfaces for executing the scripts: cscript.exe and wscript.exe. CScript executes on the command line, while WScript executes within the Windows environment. The following are elements of Windows Script Host (WSH):

o   XML Elements
o   <u>Objects</u>
o   <u>Properties</u>
o   <u>Methods</u>
o   Events
o   Error Messages

Note: This book covers information regarding WSH Objects, WSH Properties, and WSH Methods.

Windows Management Instrumentation (WMI)

Windows Management Instrumentation (WMI) is a method for providing access to management information for Windows operating system *(see <u>Windows Management</u>*

Skype: rex.jones34
Twitter: @RexJonesII
Email: <u>Rex.Jones@Test4Success.org</u>
LinkedIn: <u>https://www.linkedin.com/in/rexjones34</u>

Instrumentation (WMI) in Chapter 8.) WMI adheres to standards set by the Distributed
Management Task Force (DMTF). The standards support implementations that enable the
management of conventional or developing technologies.

Chapter 1 provides an overview of each chapter in this book. The chapters to follow are
Dictionary Objects, FileSystemObject (FSO), Classes, Regular Expressions, Debugging and
Handling Errors, Windows Script Host (WSH), and Windows Management Instrumentation
(WMI). Chapter 2 will discuss Dictionary Objects which are objects containing all types of
data.

Chapter 2
Dictionary Objects

Dictionary objects are objects that contain any type of data such as, strings, dates, arrays, and objects. Key/item pairs are used to store the data as an associative array. An associative array is provided by a Dictionary object that means each item in the array has a unique associated key. Keys can be in the form of integers or strings while an item can be integers, strings, or arrays. The following is a list of benefits for a Dictionary object:

- o Contains relevant data throughout the entire runtime
- o Associated keys make it easy to locate items
- o Key/item pairs can be removed to release memory

The following Mercury Tours Home page will be used as an example to explain Dictionary objects:

Figure 2.1 – Mercury Tours Home Page

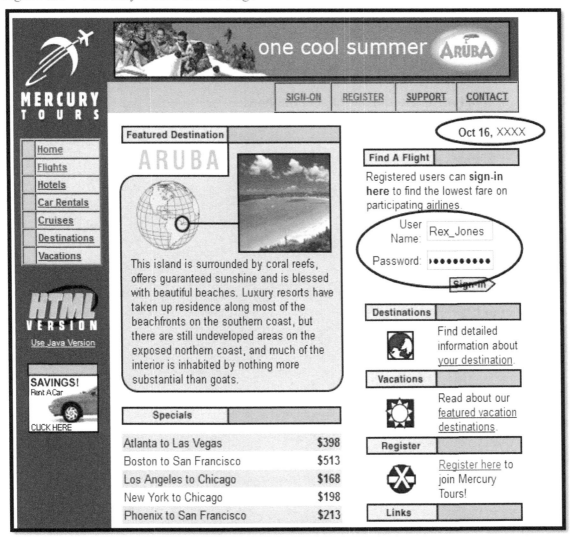

Chapter 2 will discuss the following information regarding Dictionary objects:

3 Tips To Master QTP/UFT Within 30 Days
http://tinyurl.com/3-Tips-For-QTP-UFT

Free Webinars, Videos, and Live Trainings
http://tinyurl.com/Free-QTP-UFT-Selenium

✓ Dictionary Object Methods
✓ Dictionary Object Properties

Dictionary Object Methods

The following is a list of six Dictionary Object methods:

○ Add Method
○ Exists Method
○ Items Method
○ Keys Method
○ Remove Method
○ RemoveAll Method

Add Method

An Add method adds a new key/item pair to a Dictionary object. The following is the syntax for the Add method:

Syntax
Object.Add (Key, Item)

Figure 2.2 – Add Method Syntax Details

Argument	Description
Object	Name of a Dictionary object
Key	The unique key associated with the item getting added
Item	The item associated with the key getting added

The following example utilizes the Add method:

Skype: rex.jones34
Twitter: @RexJonesII
Email: Rex.Jones@Test4Success.org
LinkedIn: https://www.linkedin.com/in/rexjones34

Chapter 2
Dictionary Objects   You Must Learn VBScript for QTP/UFT

Figure 2.3 – Screenshot of Sample Code

```
1     Option Explicit
2
3     Dim objMercuryHomePg
4
5     Set objMercuryHomePg = CreateObject("Scripting.Dictionary")
6
7     objMercuryHomePg.Add "UserName", "Rex_Jones"
8     objMercuryHomePg.Add "Password", "Rex_Jones34"
9     objMercuryHomePg.Add "Date", Date()
10
11    MsgBox "The UserName is " & objMercuryHomePg("UserName")
12    MsgBox "The Password is " & objMercuryHomePg("Password")
13    MsgBox "The Date is " & objMercuryHomePg("Date")
```

Option Explicit

Dim objMercuryHomePg

Set objMercuryHomePg = **CreateObject**("Scripting.Dictionary")

objMercuryHomePg.Add "UserName", "Rex_Jones"
objMercuryHomePg.Add "Password", "Rex_Jones34"
objMercuryHomePg.Add "Date", **Date**()

MsgBox "The UserName is " & objMercuryHomePg("UserName")
MsgBox "The Password is " & objMercuryHomePg("Password")
MsgBox "The Date is " & objMercuryHomePg("Date")

- o   The first output displays, "The UserName is Rex_Jones"
- o   The second output displays, "The Password is Rex_Jones34"

3 Tips To Master QTP/UFT Within 30 Days
http://tinyurl.com/3-Tips-For-QTP-UFT

Free Webinars, Videos, and Live Trainings
http://tinyurl.com/Free-QTP-UFT-Selenium

- o The third output displays, "The Date is 10/16/XXXX"

Figure 2.4 – Screenshots Displaying Output from Above Code

Three key/item pairs were added to the Dictionary object: "objMercuryHomePg," by using hard-coded data and a built-in function. In this case, each unique key, e.g., "UserName," represents the field name while the item, e.g., "Rex_Jones" contains data for the field.

An error occurs if a duplicate key gets added to the Dictionary object. The following is an example of a duplicate key being added to the Dictionary object:

Figure 2.5 – Screenshot of Sample Code

```
Option Explicit

Dim objMercuryHomePg

Set objMercuryHomePg = CreateObject("Scripting.Dictionary")

objMercuryHomePg.Add "UserName", "Rex_Jones"
objMercuryHomePg.Add "Password", "Rex_Jones34"
objMercuryHomePg.Add "Date", Date()
objMercuryHomePg.Add "UserName", "Rex_Jones"

MsgBox "The UserName is " & objMercuryHomePg("UserName")
MsgBox "The Password is " & objMercuryHomePg("Password")
MsgBox "The Date is " & objMercuryHomePg("Date")
```

Option Explicit

Dim objMercuryHomePg

Set objMercuryHomePg = **CreateObject**("Scripting.Dictionary")

objMercuryHomePg.Add "UserName", "Rex_Jones"
objMercuryHomePg.Add "Password", "Rex_Jones34"
objMercuryHomePg.Add "Date", **Date**()
objMercuryHomePg.Add "UserName", "Rex_Jones"

MsgBox "The UserName is " & objMercuryHomePg("UserName")
MsgBox "The Password is " & objMercuryHomePg("Password")
MsgBox "The Date is " & objMercuryHomePg("Date")

3 Tips To Master QTP/UFT Within 30 Days
http://tinyurl.com/3-Tips-For-QTP-UFT

Free Webinars, Videos, and Live Trainings
http://tinyurl.com/Free-QTP-UFT-Selenium

The output displays a Run Error "This key is already associated with an element of this collection"

Figure 2.6 – Screenshot Displaying Output from Above Code

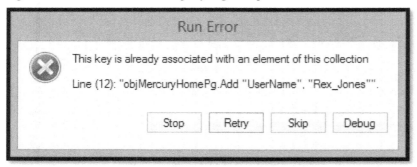

An automation engineer will not add a duplicate key near an existing key. However, it is possible for a duplicate key to be mistakenly added somewhere else in the Dictionary object script file. Dictionary objects resemble tables because a key is similar to a header and an item is similar to a row. The following screenshot displays all of the Keys and Items in Dictionary object, "objMercuryHomePg:"

Figure 2.7 – Dictionary Object Table Format

Keys	UserName	Password	Date
Items	Rex_Jones	Rex_Jones34	10/16/XXXX

Exists Method
An Exists method determines if a key exists in a specific Dictionary object. True indicates the key exists and False indicates the key does not exist, in the specified Dictionary object. The following is the syntax for Exists method:

Chapter 2
Dictionary Objects   You Must Learn VBScript for QTP/UFT

Syntax
Object.Exists (Key)

Figure 2.8 – Exists Method Syntax Details

Argument	Description
Object	Name of a Dictionary object
Key	The unique key getting searched for in the Dictionary object

The following example utilizes the Exists method:

3 Tips To Master QTP/UFT Within 30 Days
http://tinyurl.com/3-Tips-For-QTP-UFT

Free Webinars, Videos, and Live Trainings
http://tinyurl.com/Free-QTP-UFT-Selenium

Figure 2.9 – Screenshot of Sample Code

```
1   Option Explicit
2
3   Dim objMercuryHomePg
4
5   Set objMercuryHomePg = CreateObject("Scripting.Dictionary")
6
7   objMercuryHomePg.Add "UserName", "Rex_Jones"
8   objMercuryHomePg.Add "Password", "Rex_Jones34"
9   objMercuryHomePg.Add "Date", Date()
10
11  MsgBox objMercuryHomePg.Exists("UserName")
12  MsgBox objMercuryHomePg.Exists("Address")
13
14  If objMercuryHomePg.Exists("UserName") Then
15        MsgBox "UserName exists in the dictionary."
16  Else
17        MsgBox "UserName does not exist in the dictionary."
18  End If
19
20  If objMercuryHomePg.Exists("Address") Then
21        MsgBox "Address exists in the dictionary."
22  Else
23        MsgBox "Address does not exist in the dictionary."
24  End If
```

Option Explicit

Dim objMercuryHomePg

Set objMercuryHomePg = **CreateObject**("Scripting.Dictionary")

objMercuryHomePg.Add "UserName", "Rex_Jones"

Skype: rex.jones34
Twitter: @RexJonesII
Email: Rex.Jones@Test4Success.org
LinkedIn: https://www.linkedin.com/in/rexjones34

objMercuryHomePg.Add "Password", "Rex_Jones34"
objMercuryHomePg.Add "Date", **Date**()

MsgBox objMercuryHomePg.Exists("UserName")
MsgBox objMercuryHomePg.Exists("Address")

If objMercuryHomePg.Exists("UserName") **Then**
      MsgBox "UserName exists in the dictionary."
Else
      MsgBox "UserName does not exist in the dictionary."
End If

If objMercuryHomePg.Exists("Address") **Then**
      MsgBox "Address exists in the dictionary."
Else
      MsgBox "Address does not exist in the dictionary."
End If

- o The first output displays, "True"
- o The second output displays, "False"
- o The third output displays, "UserName exists in the dictionary."
- o The fourth output displays, "Address does not exist in the dictionary."

Figure 2.10 – Screenshots Displaying Output from Above Code

For demonstration purposes, the Exist methods:
MsgBox objMercuryHomePg.Exists("UserName") and
MsgBox objMercuryHomePg.Exists("Address") return True and False. The first message box returns True because UserName is added to the Dictionary object, while Address returns False because Address is not added to the Dictionary.

Usually, automation engineers utilize the Exists method within an If statement
"**If** objMercuryHomePg.Exists("UserName") …" to determine whether a key (UserName) does or does not exist.

Skype: rex.jones34
Twitter: @RexJonesII
Email: Rex.Jones@Test4Success.org
LinkedIn: https://www.linkedin.com/in/rexjones34

Chapter 2
Dictionary Objects   You Must Learn VBScript for QTP/UFT

Items Method

An Items method retrieves all of the items in a specified Dictionary object and returns the items in an array. The following is the syntax for the Items method:

Syntax
[ArrayName] = Object.Items

Figure 2.11 – Items Method Syntax Details

Argument	Description
ArrayName	Name of the array
Object	Name of a Dictionary object

The following example utilizes the Items method:

Figure 2.12 – Screenshot of Sample Code

```
1    Option Explicit
2
3    Dim i
4    Dim objMercuryHomePg
5    Dim arrMercuryHomePg
6
7    Set objMercuryHomePg = CreateObject("Scripting.Dictionary")
8
9    objMercuryHomePg.Add "UserName", "Rex_Jones"
10   objMercuryHomePg.Add "Password", "Rex_Jones34"
11   objMercuryHomePg.Add "Date", Date()
12
13   arrMercuryHomePg = objMercuryHomePg.Items
14
15   For i =0 To objMercuryHomePg.Count - 1
16       MsgBox vbCrLf & "The item is " & arrMercuryHomePg(i)
17   Next
```

Option Explicit

Dim i
Dim objMercuryHomePg
Dim arrMercuryHomePg

Set objMercuryHomePg = **CreateObject**("Scripting.Dictionary")

objMercuryHomePg.Add "UserName", "Rex_Jones"
objMercuryHomePg.Add "Password", "Rex_Jones34"
objMercuryHomePg.Add "Date", **Date**()

arrMercuryHomePg = objMercuryHomePg.Items

Skype: rex.jones34
Twitter: @RexJonesII
Email: Rex.Jones@Test4Success.org
LinkedIn: https://www.linkedin.com/in/rexjones34

For i =0 **To** objMercuryHomePg.Count - 1
   MsgBox vbCrLf & "The item is " & arrMercuryHomePg(i)
Next

- o The first output displays, "The item is Rex_Jones"
- o The second output displays, "The item is Rex_Jones34"
- o The third output displays, "The item is 10/16/XXXX"

Figure 2.13 – Screenshots Displaying Output from Above Code

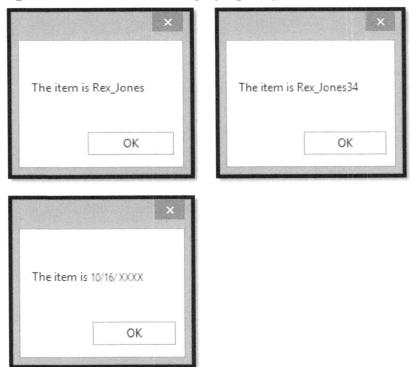

The Items method was used along with an array:
"arrMercuryHomePg = objMercuryHomePg.Items," to fetch all of the items while the
message box: "**MsgBox vbCrLf** & arrMercuryHomePg(i)" displays each item.

Keys Method

A Keys method retrieves all of the existing keys in a specified Dictionary object and return
the keys in an array. The following is the syntax for Keys method:

Syntax
[ArrayName] = Object.Keys

Figure 2.14 – Keys Method Syntax Details

Argument	Description
ArrayName	Name of the array
Object	Name of a Dictionary object

The following example utilizes the Keys method:

Skype: rex.jones34
Twitter: @RexJonesII
Email: Rex.Jones@Test4Success.org
LinkedIn: https://www.linkedin.com/in/rexjones34

Figure 2.15 – Screenshot of Sample Code

```
1    Option Explicit
2
3    Dim i
4    Dim objMercuryHomePg
5    Dim arrMercuryHomePg
6
7    Set objMercuryHomePg = CreateObject("Scripting.Dictionary")
8
9    objMercuryHomePg.Add "UserName", "Rex_Jones"
10   objMercuryHomePg.Add "Password", "Rex_Jones34"
11   objMercuryHomePg.Add "Date", Date()
12
13   arrMercuryHomePg = objMercuryHomePg.Keys
14
15   For i =0 To objMercuryHomePg.Count - 1
16       MsgBox vbCrLf & "The key is " & arrMercuryHomePg(i)
17   Next
```

Option Explicit

Dim i
Dim objMercuryHomePg
Dim arrMercuryHomePg

Set objMercuryHomePg = **CreateObject**("Scripting.Dictionary")

objMercuryHomePg.Add "UserName", "Rex_Jones"
objMercuryHomePg.Add "Password", "Rex_Jones34"
objMercuryHomePg.Add "Date", **Date**()

arrMercuryHomePg = objMercuryHomePg.Keys

3 Tips To Master QTP/UFT Within 30 Days
http://tinyurl.com/3-Tips-For-QTP-UFT

Free Webinars, Videos, and Live Trainings
http://tinyurl.com/Free-QTP-UFT-Selenium

For i =0 **To** objMercuryHomePg.Count - 1
    MsgBox vbCrLf & "The key is " & arrMercuryHomePg(i)
Next

- o The first output displays, "The key is UserName"
- o The second output displays, "The key is Password"
- o The third output displays, "The key is Date"

Figure 2.16 – Screenshots Displaying Output from Above Code

The Keys method is used along with an array:
"arrMercuryHomePg = objMercuryHomePg.Keys" to get all of the keys, while the message
box "**MsgBox vbCrLf** & arrMercuryHomePg(i)" displays each key.

Remove Method
A Remove method removes a single key/item pair from the specified Dictionary object by
using the key. The following is the syntax for Remove method:

Syntax
Object.Remove(Key)

Figure 2.17 – Remove Method Syntax Details

Argument	Description
Object	Name of a Dictionary object
Key	The associated key that will remove a particular key/item pair from the Dictionary object

The following example utilizes the Remove method:

Figure 2.18 – Screenshot of Sample Code

```
1   Option Explicit
2
3   Dim i
4   Dim objMercuryHomePg
5   Dim arrMercuryHomePg
6
7   Set objMercuryHomePg = CreateObject("Scripting.Dictionary")
8
9   objMercuryHomePg.Add "UserName", "Rex_Jones"
10  objMercuryHomePg.Add "Password", "Rex_Jones34"
11  objMercuryHomePg.Add "Date", Date()
12
13  objMercuryHomePg.Remove("Date")
14
15  arrMercuryHomePg = objMercuryHomePg.Keys
16
17  For i =0 To objMercuryHomePg.Count - 1
18      MsgBox vbCrLf & "The key is " & arrMercuryHomePg(i)
19  Next
```

3 Tips To Master QTP/UFT Within 30 Days
http://tinyurl.com/3-Tips-For-QTP-UFT

Free Webinars, Videos, and Live Trainings
http://tinyurl.com/Free-QTP-UFT-Selenium

Chapter 2
Dictionary Objects   You Must Learn VBScript for QTP/UFT

Option Explicit

Dim i
Dim objMercuryHomePg
Dim arrMercuryHomePg

Set objMercuryHomePg = **CreateObject**("Scripting.Dictionary")

objMercuryHomePg.Add "UserName", "Rex_Jones"
objMercuryHomePg.Add "Password", "Rex_Jones34"
objMercuryHomePg.Add "Date", **Date**()

objMercuryHomePg.Remove("Date")

arrMercuryHomePg = objMercuryHomePg.Keys

For i =0 **To** objMercuryHomePg.Count - 1
    MsgBox vbCrLf & "The key is " & arrMercuryHomePg(i)
Next

- o   The first output displays, "The key is UserName"
- o   The second output displays, "The key is Password"

Skype: rex.jones34
Twitter: @RexJonesII
Email: Rex.Jones@Test4Success.org
LinkedIn: https://www.linkedin.com/in/rexjones34

Figure 2.19 – Screenshots Displaying Output from Above Code

The Date Dictionary object was removed when using the Remove method.

RemoveAll Method

A RemoveAll method removes all key/item pairs from the specified Dictionary object. The following is the syntax for the RemoveAll method:

Syntax
Object.RemoveAll

Figure 2.20 – Remove Method Syntax Details

Argument	Description
Object	Name of a Dictionary object

The following example utilizes the RemoveAll method:

Figure 2.21 – Screenshot of Sample Code

```
1    Option Explicit
2
3    Dim i
4    Dim objMercuryHomePg
5    Dim arrMercuryHomePg
6
7    Set objMercuryHomePg = CreateObject("Scripting.Dictionary")
8
9    objMercuryHomePg.Add "UserName", "Rex_Jones"
10   objMercuryHomePg.Add "Password", "Rex_Jones34"
11   objMercuryHomePg.Add "Date", Date()
12
13   objMercuryHomePg.RemoveAll
14
15   objMercuryHomePg.Add "Test", "All key-item pairs before the RemoveAll method has been cleared."
16
17   arrMercuryHomePg = objMercuryHomePg.Items
18
19   For i =0 To objMercuryHomePg.Count - 1
20       MsgBox vbCrLf & "The key is " & arrMercuryHomePg(i)
21   Next
```

Option Explicit

Dim i
Dim objMercuryHomePg
Dim arrMercuryHomePg

Set objMercuryHomePg = **CreateObject**("Scripting.Dictionary")

objMercuryHomePg.Add "UserName", "Rex_Jones"
objMercuryHomePg.Add "Password", "Rex_Jones34"
objMercuryHomePg.Add "Date", **Date**()

objMercuryHomePg.RemoveAll

Skype: rex.jones34
Twitter: @RexJonesII
Email: Rex.Jones@Test4Success.org
LinkedIn: https://www.linkedin.com/in/rexjones34

objMercuryHomePg.Add "Test", "All key-item pairs before the RemoveAll method has been cleared."

arrMercuryHomePg = objMercuryHomePg.Items

For i =0 **To** objMercuryHomePg.Count - 1
   MsgBox vbCrLf & "The key is " & arrMercuryHomePg(i)
Next

The output displays, "All key-item pairs before the RemoveAll method has been cleared."

Figure 2.22 – Screenshots Displaying Output from Above Code

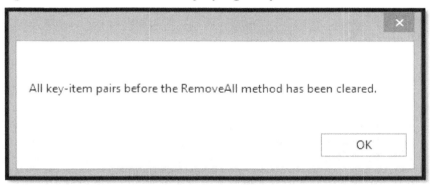

The RemoveAll method clears all of the key/item pairs, except for the unique key "Test." This key is added after all of the previous key/item pairs are removed.

Dictionary Object Properties

The following is a list of four Dictionary object properties:

- o Count Property
- o Item Property

3 Tips To Master QTP/UFT Within 30 Days
http://tinyurl.com/3-Tips-For-QTP-UFT

Free Webinars, Videos, and Live Trainings
http://tinyurl.com/Free-QTP-UFT-Selenium

- o <u>Key Property</u>
- o <u>CompareMode Property</u>

Count Property

A Count property returns the number of key/item pairs in the specified Dictionary object. The following is the syntax for the Count property:

Syntax
Object.Count

Figure 2.23 – Count Property Syntax Details

Argument	Description
Object	Name of an object

The following example utilizes the Count property:

Figure 2.24 – Screenshot of Sample Code

```
1    Option Explicit
2
3    Dim objMercuryHomePg
4
5    Set objMercuryHomePg = CreateObject("Scripting.Dictionary")
6
7    objMercuryHomePg.Add "UserName", "Rex_Jones"
8    objMercuryHomePg.Add "Password", "Rex_Jones34"
9    objMercuryHomePg.Add "Date", Date()
10
11   MsgBox "There are " & objMercuryHomePg.Count & " key-item pairs."
12
```

Option Explicit

Dim objMercuryHomePg

Set objMercuryHomePg = **CreateObject**("Scripting.Dictionary")

objMercuryHomePg.Add "UserName", "Rex_Jones"
objMercuryHomePg.Add "Password", "Rex_Jones34"
objMercuryHomePg.Add "Date", **Date**()

MsgBox "There are " & objMercuryHomePg.Count & " key-item pairs."

The output displays "There are 3 key-item pairs."

Figure 2.25 – Screenshot Displaying Output from Above Code

The Count property returns the number "3," that represents each key/item pair added to the Dictionary object: "objMercuryHomePg."

Item Property
An Item property is used to set or return an item for a specific key in a Dictionary object. This property can be used in three ways:

1. To add a new item
2. To read or return the value of an existing item
3. To update the value of an existing item

The following is the syntax for the Item property:

Syntax
Object.Item(Key) [= NewItem]

Figure 2.26 – Item Property Syntax Details

Argument	Description
Object	Name of an object
Key	Key associated with the item being returned or added
NewItem	New value for the specified key

The following example shows how to add, update, and return an item utilizing the Item property:

Skype: rex.jones34
Twitter: @RexJonesII
Email: Rex.Jones@Test4Success.org
LinkedIn: https://www.linkedin.com/in/rexjones34

Figure 2.27 – Screenshot of Sample Code

```
1    Option Explicit
2
3    Dim strUserName
4    Dim objMercuryHomePg
5
6    Set objMercuryHomePg = CreateObject("Scripting.Dictionary")
7
8    'Add and Display New item
9    objMercuryHomePg.Item("UserName") = "James_Jones"
10   MsgBox objMercuryHomePg("UserName") & " has been added"
11
12   'Update and Display the item
13   objMercuryHomePg.Item("UserName") = "James_Allen"
14   MsgBox objMercuryHomePg("UserName") & " updates the previous UserName"
15
16   'Return and Display the item
17   strUserName = objMercuryHomePg.Item("UserName")
18   MsgBox "The updated Username " & strUserName & " is returned"
```

Option Explicit

Dim strUserName
Dim objMercuryHomePg

Set objMercuryHomePg = **CreateObject**("Scripting.Dictionary")

'Add and Display New item
objMercuryHomePg.Item("UserName") = "James_Jones"
MsgBox objMercuryHomePg("UserName") & " has been added"

'Update and Display the item

3 Tips To Master QTP/UFT Within 30 Days
http://tinyurl.com/3-Tips-For-QTP-UFT

Free Webinars, Videos, and Live Trainings
http://tinyurl.com/Free-QTP-UFT-Selenium

objMercuryHomePg.Item("UserName") = "James_Allen"
MsgBox objMercuryHomePg("UserName") & " updates the previous UserName"

'Return and Display the item
strUserName = objMercuryHomePg.Item("UserName")
MsgBox "The updated Username " & strUserName & " is returned"

- o   The first output displays, "James_Jones has been added"
- o   The second output displays, "James_Allen updates the previous UserName"
- o   The third output displays, "The updated Username James_Allen is returned"

Figure 2.28 – Screenshots Displaying Output from Above Code

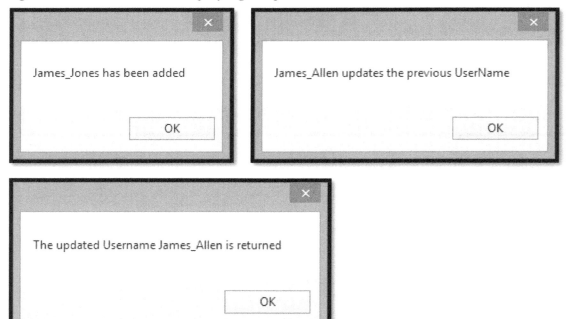

As mentioned, the Item property can be used to add, update, or return an item. It is important to use the Exists method when updating or returning an item. If the specified key is not located when attempting to update the item then a new key is added with an item value. However, a new key is added without an item value if the specified key is not located when attempting to return the item. The following are three modes used to add an item to a Dictionary object:

1. objMercuryHomePg.Add "UserName", "Rex_Jones"
2. objMercuryHomePg.Item("UserName") = "Rex_Jones"
3. objMercuryHomePg("UserName") = "Rex_Jones"

Modes one and two have already been discussed. The first example uses the Add method, which is the most explicit syntax, while the second example uses the Item property. Item property is the default property, so referring to the name is optional. An omission of the name "Item" creates the third mode.

Key Property

A Key property sets the value of an existing key in a Dictionary object. The following is the syntax for Key property:

Syntax
Object.Key(ExistingKey) = NewKey

Figure 2.29 – Key Property Syntax Details

Argument	Description
Object	Name of a Dictionary object
ExistingKey	Value of existing key
NewKey	New key value that replaces the existing key. If an existing key is not located, then a new key is created with an associated empty item

3 Tips To Master QTP/UFT Within 30 Days
http://tinyurl.com/3-Tips-For-QTP-UFT

Free Webinars, Videos, and Live Trainings
http://tinyurl.com/Free-QTP-UFT-Selenium

The following example utilizes the Key property:

Figure 2.30 – Screenshot of Sample Code

```
1    Option Explicit
2
3    Dim i
4    Dim objMercuryHomePg
5    Dim arrMercuryHomePg
6
7    Set objMercuryHomePg = CreateObject("Scripting.Dictionary")
8
9    objMercuryHomePg.Add "UserName", "Rex_Jones"
10   objMercuryHomePg.Add "Password", "Rex_Jones34"
11   objMercuryHomePg.Add "Date", Date()
12
13   arrMercuryHomePg = objMercuryHomePg.Keys
14
15   For i =0 To objMercuryHomePg.Count - 1
16       MsgBox vbCrLf & "Key value is " & arrMercuryHomePg(i)
17   Next
18
19   objMercuryHomePg.Key("Date") = "TodaysDate"
20
21   arrMercuryHomePg = objMercuryHomePg.Keys
22
23   For i =0 To objMercuryHomePg.Count - 1
24       MsgBox vbCrLf & "Key value is " & arrMercuryHomePg(i)
25   Next
```

Option Explicit

Dim i
Dim objMercuryHomePg
Dim arrMercuryHomePg

Skype: rex.jones34
Twitter: @RexJonesII
Email: Rex.Jones@Test4Success.org
LinkedIn: https://www.linkedin.com/in/rexjones34

```
Set objMercuryHomePg = CreateObject("Scripting.Dictionary")

objMercuryHomePg.Add "UserName", "Rex_Jones"
objMercuryHomePg.Add "Password", "Rex_Jones34"
objMercuryHomePg.Add "Date", Date()

arrMercuryHomePg = objMercuryHomePg.Keys

For i =0 To objMercuryHomePg.Count - 1
    MsgBox vbCrLf & "Key value is " & arrMercuryHomePg(i)
Next

objMercuryHomePg.Key("Date") = "TodaysDate"

arrMercuryHomePg = objMercuryHomePg.Keys

For i =0 To objMercuryHomePg.Count - 1
    MsgBox vbCrLf & "Key value is " & arrMercuryHomePg(i)
Next
```

- o The first output displays, "Key value is UserName"
- o The second output displays, "Key value is Password"
- o The third output displays, "Key value is Date"
- o The fourth output displays, "Key value is UserName"
- o The fifth output displays, "Key value is Password"
- o The sixth output displays, "Key value is TodaysDate"

3 Tips To Master QTP/UFT Within 30 Days
http://tinyurl.com/3-Tips-For-QTP-UFT

Free Webinars, Videos, and Live Trainings
http://tinyurl.com/Free-QTP-UFT-Selenium

Figure 2.31 – Screenshots Displaying Output from Above Code

Skype: rex.jones34
Twitter: @RexJonesII
Email: Rex.Jones@Test4Success.org
LinkedIn: https://www.linkedin.com/in/rexjones34

The third screenshot displays the existing key value (Date), while the sixth screenshot displays the new key value (TodaysDate).

CompareMode Property

A CompareMode property sets or returns the comparison mode for comparing key values in a Dictionary object. Keys can be considered as case-sensitive or case-insensitive. The following is the syntax for the CompareMode property:

Syntax
Object.CompareMode [= CompareConstant]

Figure 2.32 – CompareMode Property Syntax Details

Argument	Description
Object	Name of a Dictionary object
CompareConstant	The value representing the comparison mode

Figure 2.33 – CompareConstants

Constant	Value	Description
VBBinaryCompare	0	Binary Comparison
VBTextCompare	1	Text Comparison
VBDataBaseCompare	2	Database information comparison

The following example utilizes the CompareMode property via VBTextCompare:

3 Tips To Master QTP/UFT Within 30 Days
http://tinyurl.com/3-Tips-For-QTP-UFT

Free Webinars, Videos, and Live Trainings
http://tinyurl.com/Free-QTP-UFT-Selenium

Figure 2.34 – Screenshot of Sample Code

```
1   Option Explicit
2
3   Dim i
4   Dim objMercuryHomePg
5   Dim arrMercuryHomePg
6
7   Set objMercuryHomePg = CreateObject("Scripting.Dictionary")
8
9   'The value '1' or CompareConstant 'VBTextCompare' can be used
10  objMercuryHomePg.CompareMode = VBTextCompare
11
12  objMercuryHomePg.Add "UserName", "Rex_Jones"
13  objMercuryHomePg.Add "Password", "Rex_Jones34"
14  objMercuryHomePg.Add "Date", Date()
15  objMercuryHomePg.Add "DATE", Date()
16
17  arrMercuryHomePg = objMercuryHomePg.Keys
18
19  For i =0 To objMercuryHomePg.Count - 1
20      MsgBox vbCrLf & "The unique key is " & arrMercuryHomePg(i)
21  Next
```

Option Explicit

Dim i
Dim objMercuryHomePg
Dim arrMercuryHomePg

Set objMercuryHomePg = **CreateObject**("Scripting.Dictionary")

'The value '1' or CompareConstant 'VBTextCompare' can be used
objMercuryHomePg.CompareMode = **VBTextCompare**

Skype: rex.jones34
Twitter: @RexJonesII
Email: Rex.Jones@Test4Success.org
LinkedIn: https://www.linkedin.com/in/rexjones34

objMercuryHomePg.Add "UserName", "Rex_Jones"
objMercuryHomePg.Add "Password", "Rex_Jones34"
objMercuryHomePg.Add "Date", **Date**()
objMercuryHomePg.Add "DATE", **Date**()

arrMercuryHomePg = objMercuryHomePg.Keys

For i =0 **To** objMercuryHomePg.Count - 1
  MsgBox vbCrLf & "The unique key is " & arrMercuryHomePg(i)
Next

The output displays a Run Error: "This key is already associated with an element of this collection"

Figure 2.35 – Screenshot Displaying Output from Above Code

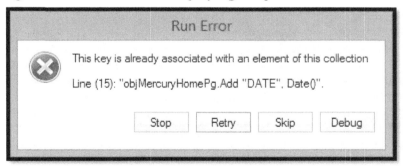

An error appeared due to the CompareConstant, "VBTextCompare," which is case-insensitive. Case-insensitive means that the program did not distinguish a difference between uppercase and lowercase letters (i.e., Date and DATE). The following is an example utilizing CompareMode property via VBBinaryCompare:

3 Tips To Master QTP/UFT Within 30 Days
http://tinyurl.com/3-Tips-For-QTP-UFT

Free Webinars, Videos, and Live Trainings
http://tinyurl.com/Free-QTP-UFT-Selenium

Figure 2.36 – Screenshot of Sample Code

```
1   Option Explicit
2
3   Dim i
4   Dim objMercuryHomePg
5   Dim arrMercuryHomePg
6
7   Set objMercuryHomePg = CreateObject("Scripting.Dictionary")
8
9   'The value '0' or CompareConstant 'VBBinaryCompare' can be used
10  objMercuryHomePg.CompareMode = VBBinaryCompare
11
12  objMercuryHomePg.Add "UserName", "Rex_Jones"
13  objMercuryHomePg.Add "Password", "Rex_Jones34"
14  objMercuryHomePg.Add "Date", Date()
15  objMercuryHomePg.Add "DATE", Date()
16
17  arrMercuryHomePg = objMercuryHomePg.Keys
18
19  For i = 0 To objMercuryHomePg.Count - 1
20      MsgBox vbCrLf & "The unique key is " & arrMercuryHomePg(i)
21  Next
```

Option Explicit

Dim i
Dim objMercuryHomePg
Dim arrMercuryHomePg

Set objMercuryHomePg = **CreateObject**("Scripting.Dictionary")

'The value '0' or CompareConstant 'VBBinaryCompare' can be used

Skype: rex.jones34
Twitter: @RexJonesII
Email: Rex.Jones@Test4Success.org
LinkedIn: https://www.linkedin.com/in/rexjones34

objMercuryHomePg.CompareMode = **VBBinaryCompare**

objMercuryHomePg.Add "UserName", "Rex_Jones"
objMercuryHomePg.Add "Password", "Rex_Jones34"
objMercuryHomePg.Add "Date", **Date()**
objMercuryHomePg.Add "DATE", **Date()**

arrMercuryHomePg = objMercuryHomePg.Keys

For i = 0 **To** objMercuryHomePg.Count - 1
    MsgBox vbCrLf & "The unique key is " & arrMercuryHomePg(i)
Next

- o   The first output displays, "The unique key is UserName"
- o   The second output displays, "The unique key is Password"
- o   The third output displays, "The unique key is Date"
- o   The fourth output displays, "The unique key is DATE"

Figure 2.37 – Screenshots Displaying Output from Above Code

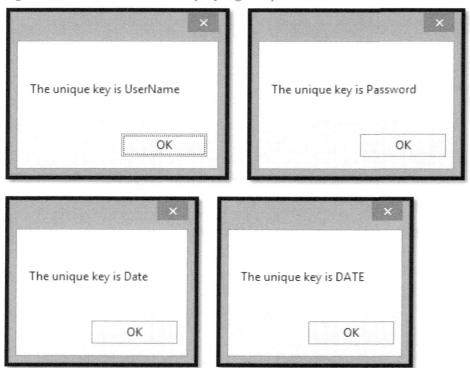

An error did not appear because CompareConstant "i.e., VBBinaryCompare" is case-sensitive. Case-sensitive means that the program recognizes a difference between uppercase and lowercase letters (i.e., Date and DATE).

Chapter 2 explained the concepts of key/item pairs, Dictionary Object methods and properties. Key/item pairs store data as an associative array. Dictionary Objects possess six methods and four properties. Chapter 3 covers FileSystemObject (FSO), which allows the file system to be accessed and manipulated.

Skype: rex.jones34
Twitter: @RexJonesII
Email: Rex.Jones@Test4Success.org
LinkedIn: https://www.linkedin.com/in/rexjones34

Chapter 3
FileSystemObject (FSO)

The FileSystemObject (FSO) hierarchy collaborate with each other to access and manipulate the file system. Files and folders can be created, read, or located via test scripts. In addition, FSO can retrieve information regarding drives associated to the computer system.

Chapter 3 will cover the following regarding FileSystemObject (FSO):

- ✓ FSO Objects
- ✓ FSO Collections
- ✓ Methods
- ✓ Properties

FSO Objects

FSO objects provide object-oriented access to files and directories. The following is a list of FSO objects:

- o Drive Object
- o File Object
- o FileSystemObject Object
- o Folder Object
- o TextStream Object

Drive Object

The Drive object provides information regarding a network share or drives connected to a system. This object has zero methods and 12 properties:

3 Tips To Master QTP/UFT Within 30 Days
http://tinyurl.com/3-Tips-For-QTP-UFT

Free Webinars, Videos, and Live Trainings
http://tinyurl.com/Free-QTP-UFT-Selenium

Drive Object Properties
The following are properties for Drive object:

Figure 3.1 – Drive Object Properties

AvailableSpace	Path
DriveLetter	RootFolder
DriveType	SerialNumber
FileSystem	ShareName
FreeSpace	TotalSize
IsReady	VolumeName

File Object

The File object provides access to all of the file properties. This object has four methods and 12 properties:

File Object Methods
The following are methods for File object:

1. Copy
2. Delete
3. Move
4. OpenAsTextStream

File Object Properties
The following are properties for File object:

Figure 3.2 – File Object Properties

Attributes	ParentFolder
DateCreated	Path
DateLastAccessed	ShortName
DateLastModified	ShortPath
Drive	Size
Name	Type

Skype: rex.jones34
Twitter: @RexJonesII
Email: Rex.Jones@Test4Success.org
LinkedIn: https://www.linkedin.com/in/rexjones34

FileSystemObject Object

The FileSystemObject (FSO) object represents the root object of the FSO object model which is a hierarchy of Component Object Model (COM) objects. In other words, the FSO object provides a way to access and manipulate the entire computer file system. This object has 26 methods and one property:

FileSystemObject Methods
The following are methods for FileSystemObject:

Figure 3.3 – FileSystemObject Methods

BuildPath	GetDriveName
CopyFile	GetExtensionName
CopyFolder	GetFile
CreateFolder	GetFileVersion
CreateTextFile	GetFileName
DeleteFile	GetFolder
DeleteFolder	GetParentFolderName
DriveExists	GetSpecialFolder
FileExists	GetStandardStream
FolderExists	GetTempName
GetAbsolutePathName	MoveFile
GetBaseName	MoveFolder
GetDrive	OpenTextFile

FileSystemObject Property
The following is a property for FileSystemObject:

o   Drives

3 Tips To Master QTP/UFT Within 30 Days
http://tinyurl.com/3-Tips-For-QTP-UFT

Free Webinars, Videos, and Live Trainings
http://tinyurl.com/Free-QTP-UFT-Selenium

Chapter 3
FileSystemObject (FSO)   You Must Learn VBScript for QTP/UFT

Folder Object

The Folder object provides a way to access and manipulate all of the folder properties. This object has four methods and 15 properties:

Folder Object Methods

The following are methods for Folder Object:

1. Copy
2. Delete
3. Move
4. CreateTextFile

Folder Object Properties

The following are properties for Folder Object:

Figure 3.4 – Folder Object Properties

Attributes	ParentFolder
DateCreated	Path
DateLastAccessed	ShortName
DateLastModified	ShortPath
Drive	Size
Files	SubFolders
IsRootFolder	Type
Name	

TextStream Object

The TextStream object serves as a stream of text from a text file within a file system. This object has nine methods and four properties:

TextStream Object Methods

The following are methods for TextStream Object:

Skype: rex.jones34
Twitter: @RexJonesII
Email: Rex.Jones@Test4Success.org
LinkedIn: https://www.linkedin.com/in/rexjones34

Figure 3.5 – TextStream Object Methods

Close	SkipLine
Read	Write
ReadAll	WriteBlankLines
ReadLine	WriteLine
Skip	

TextStream Object Properties
The following are properties for TextStream Object:

1. AtEndOfLine
2. AtEndOfStream
3. Column
4. Line

FSO Collections

An FSO collection is a special type of object that stores a collection of information. All of the FSO collections possess a Count and Item property. The following is a list of FSO collections:

o Drives Collection
o Files Collection
o Folders Collection

Drives Collection
The Drives collection is a read-only collection of all drives connected to the current machine. This collection has zero methods and two properties:

3 Tips To Master QTP/UFT Within 30 Days
http://tinyurl.com/3-Tips-For-QTP-UFT

Free Webinars, Videos, and Live Trainings
http://tinyurl.com/Free-QTP-UFT-Selenium

Chapter 3
FileSystemObject (FSO)   You Must Learn VBScript for QTP/UFT

Drives Collection Properties
1. Count
2. Item

Files Collection
The Files collection is a read-only collection of all File objects within a folder. This collection has zero methods and two properties:

Files Collection Properties
1. Count
2. Item

Folders Collection
The Folders collection is a collection of all Folder objects contained within a Folder object. This collection has one method and two properties:

Folders Collection Method
1. Add

Folders Collection Properties
1. Count
2. Item

Methods
The following is a list of methods in alphabetical order for all FSO objects and collections. Some of the methods are applicable to multiple objects and/or collections:

Figure 3.6 – List of Objects and Collections

Object	Collection
Drive	Drives
File	Files

Skype: rex.jones34
Twitter: @RexJonesII
Email: Rex.Jones@Test4Success.org
LinkedIn: https://www.linkedin.com/in/rexjones34

FileSystemObject	Folders
Folder	
TextStream	

The explanation of each method briefly states its associated object and/or collection along with its syntax:

Figure 3.7 – List of Methods

Add	GetFileName
BuildPath	GetFileVersion
Close	GetFolder
Copy	GetParentFolderName
CopyFile	GetSpecialFolder
CopyFolder	GetStandardStream
CreateFolder	GetTempName
CreateTextFile	Move
Delete	MoveFile
DeleteFile	MoveFolder
DeleteFolder	OpenAsTextStream
DriveExists	OpenTextFile
FileExists	Read
FolderExists	ReadAll
GetAbsolutePathName	ReadLine
GetBaseName	Skip
GetDrive	SkipLine
GetDriveName	Write
GetExtensionName	WriteBlankLines
GetFile	WriteLine

Add

An Add method adds a new folder to a Folders collection. The following is the syntax for Add method:

Syntax
Object.Add (FolderName)

Figure 3.8 – Add Method Syntax Details

Argument	Description
Object	Name of a Folders collection.
FolderName	The new folder name that will be added.

BuildPath

A BuildPath method attaches a name onto an existing path. The following is the syntax for BuildPath method:

Syntax
Object.BuildPath (Path, Name)

Figure 3.9 – BuildPath Method Syntax Details

Argument	Description
Object	Name of a FileSystemObject.
Path	The existing path to which the name is attached.
Name	Name being attached to the existing path.

Close

A Close method closes the currently open TextStream file. The following is the syntax for Close property:

Syntax
Object.Close ()

Skype: rex.jones34
Twitter: @RexJonesII
Email: Rex.Jones@Test4Success.org
LinkedIn: https://www.linkedin.com/in/rexjones34

Figure 3.10 – Close Method Syntax Details

Argument	Description
Object	Name of a TextStream object.

Copy

A Copy method copies the specified file or folder from one location (source) to another location (destination). The following is the syntax for Copy method:

Syntax
Object.Copy (Destination [, OverWrite])

Figure 3.11 – Copy Method Syntax Details

Argument	Description
Object	Name of a File or Folder object.
Destination	Character string destination which is the location to where the file or folder will be copied. Wildcard characters are not allowed.
OverWrite	Boolean value that specifies if existing file(s) or folder(s) will be overwritten. The default value is True. True: Indicates the file(s) or folder(s) are overwritten. False: Indicates the file(s) or folder(s) are not overwritten.

CopyFile

A CopyFile method copies one or more files from one location (source) to another location (destination). The following is the syntax for CopyFile method:

Syntax
Object.CopyFile (Source, Destination [, OverWrite])

Figure 3.12 – CopyFile Method Syntax Details

Argument	Description

3 Tips To Master QTP/UFT Within 30 Days
http://tinyurl.com/3-Tips-For-QTP-UFT

Free Webinars, Videos, and Live Trainings
http://tinyurl.com/Free-QTP-UFT-Selenium

Object	Name of a FileSystemObject.
Source	Location of one or more files to be copied. Character string file specification which can include wildcard characters.
Destination	Character string destination which is the location to where one or more files from source will be copied. Wildcard characters are not allowed.
OverWrite	Boolean value that specifies if existing file(s) will be overwritten. The default value is True. True: Indicates the file(s) are overwritten. False: Indicates the file(s) are not overwritten.

CopyFolder

A CopyFolder method copies one or more folders and all contents from one location (source) to another location (destination). The following is the syntax for CopyFolder method:

Syntax
Object.CopyFolder (Source, Destination [, OverWrite])

Figure 3.13 – CopyFolder Method Syntax Details

Argument	Description
Object	Name of a FileSystemObject.
Source	Location of one or more folders to be copied. Character string folder specification which can include wildcard characters.
Destination	Character string destination which is the location to where the folders and subfolders from source will be copied. Wildcard characters are not allowed.
OverWrite	Boolean value that specifies if existing folder(s) will be overwritten. The default value is True. True: Indicates the file(s) are overwritten. False: Indicates the file(s) are not overwritten.

CreateFolder

A CreateFolder method creates a folder. The following is the syntax for CreateFolder method:

Syntax
Object.CreateFolder (FolderName)

Figure 3.14 – CreateFolder Method Syntax Details

Argument	Description
Object	Name of a FileSystemObject.
FolderName	The name of the new folder that will be created.

CreateTextFile

A CreateTextFile method creates a text file and returns a TextStream object which can be used to write to a file and read from the file. The following is the syntax for CreateTextFile method:

Syntax
Object.CreateTextFile (FileName [, OverWrite [, Unicode]])

Figure 3.15 – CreateTextFile Method Syntax Details

Argument	Description
Object	Name of a FileSystemObject or Folder object.
FileName	The name of a new file that will be created.
OverWrite	Boolean value that specifies if an existing file will be overwritten. The default value is True. True: Indicates the file(s) are overwritten. False: Indicates the file(s) are not overwritten.
Unicode	Boolean value that specifies if the file is created as Unicode or ASCII. The default file is ASCII. True: Indicates the file is created as Unicode. False: Indicates the file is created as ASCII.

Delete

A Delete property deletes a specified file or folder. The following is the syntax for Delete method:

3 Tips To Master QTP/UFT Within 30 Days
http://tinyurl.com/3-Tips-For-QTP-UFT

Free Webinars, Videos, and Live Trainings
http://tinyurl.com/Free-QTP-UFT-Selenium

Syntax
Object.Delete (Force)

Figure 3.16 – Delete Method Syntax Details

Argument	Description
Object	Name of a File or Folder object.
Force	Boolean value that defaults to False. True: Permits the file(s) or folder(s) with read-only attributes to be deleted. False: Will not delete the file(s) or folder(s) with read-only attributes.

DeleteFile

A DeleteFile method deletes a specified file or files (using wildcards). The following is the syntax for DeleteFile method:

Syntax
Object.DeleteFile (File [, Force])

Figure 3.17 – DeleteFile Method Syntax Details

Argument	Description
Object	Name of a FileSystemObject.
File	The name of the file that will be deleted.
Force	Boolean value that defaults to False. True: Permits the file(s) with read-only attributes to be deleted. False: Will not delete the file(s) with read-only attributes.

DeleteFolder

A DeleteFolder method deletes a folder and its contents. The following is the syntax for DeleteFolder method:

Syntax
Object.DeleteFolder (Folder [, Force])

Skype: rex.jones34
Twitter: @RexJonesII
Email: Rex.Jones@Test4Success.org
LinkedIn: https://www.linkedin.com/in/rexjones34

Figure 3.18 – DeleteFolder Method Syntax Details

Argument	Description
Object	Name of a FileSystemObject.
Folder	The name of the folder that will be deleted.
Force	Boolean value that defaults to False. True: Permits the folder(s) with read-only attributes to be deleted. False: Will not delete the folder(s) with read-only attributes.

DriveExists

A DriveExists method verifies if a specific drive exists. True indicates the drive exists while False indicates the drive does not exist. The following is the syntax for DriveExists method:

Syntax

Object.DriveExists (Drive)

Figure 3.19 – DriveExists Method Syntax Details

Argument	Description
Object	Name of a FileSystemObject.
Drive	The drive letter or complete path.

FileExists

A FileExists method verifies if a specific file exists. True indicates the file exists while False indicates the file does not exist. The following is the syntax for FileExists method:

Syntax

Object.FileExists (File)

Figure 3.20 – FileExists Method Syntax Details

Argument	Description
Object	Name of a FileSystemObject.
File	The file name to be determined if it exist or does not exist.

FolderExists

A FolderExists method verifies if a specific folder exists. True indicates the folder exists while False indicates the folder does not exist. The following is the syntax for FolderExists method:

Syntax
Object.FolderExists (Folder)

Figure 3.21 – FolderExists Method Syntax Details

Argument	Description
Object	Name of a FileSystemObject.
Folder	The folder name to be determined if it exist or does not exist.

GetAbsolutePathName

A GetAbsolutePathName method returns the complete path from the drive's root for a path specification. The following is the syntax for GetAbsolutePathName method:

Syntax
Obect.GetAbsolutePathName (Path)

Figure 3.22 – GetAbsolutePathName Method Syntax Details

Argument	Description
Object	Name of a FileSystemObject.
Path	Path specification to change a complete and unambiguous path.

GetBaseName

A GetBaseName method returns the base name of a file or folder in a specified path. The following is the syntax for GetBaseName method:

Syntax
Object.GetBaseName (Path)

Skype: rex.jones34
Twitter: @RexJonesII
Email: Rex.Jones@Test4Success.org
LinkedIn: https://www.linkedin.com/in/rexjones34

Figure 3.23 – GetBaseName Method Syntax Details

Argument	Description
Object	Name of a FileSystemObject.
Path	The path whose base name will be returned.

GetDrive

A GetDrive method returns a Drive object corresponding to the drive in a specified path. The following is the syntax for GetDrive method:

Syntax
Object.GetDrive (Drive)

Figure 3.24 – GetDrive Method Syntax Details

Argument	Description
Object	Name of a FileSystemObject.
Drive	The drive can be one of the following: 1. Drive Letter "C" 2. Drive Letter with a colon "C:" 3. Drive Letter with a colon and path separator "C:\" 4. Network share specification "\\computer2\share1"

GetDriveName

A GetDriveName method returns the name of the drive in a specified path. The following is the syntax for GetDriveName method:

Syntax
Object.GetDriveName (Path)

Figure 3.25 – GetDriveName Method Syntax Details

Argument	Description
Object	Name of a FileSystemObject.
Path	The path whose drive name will be returned.

3 Tips To Master QTP/UFT Within 30 Days
http://tinyurl.com/3-Tips-For-QTP-UFT

Free Webinars, Videos, and Live Trainings
http://tinyurl.com/Free-QTP-UFT-Selenium

GetExtensionName

A GetExtensionName method returns the extension name of the last component in a specified path. The following is the syntax for GetExtensionName method:

Syntax
Object.GetExtensionName (Path)

Figure 3.26 – GetExtensionName Method Syntax Details

Argument	Description
Object	Name of a FileSystemObject.
Path	The path whose extension will be returned.

GetFile

A GetFile method returns a File object for the specified file name. The following is the syntax for GetFile method:

Syntax
Object.GetFile (File)

Figure 3.27 – GetFile Method Syntax Details

Argument	Description
Object	Name of a FileSystemObject.
File	The path to a specific file.

GetFileName

A GetFileName method returns the name of the last file or folder of the specified path. The following is the syntax for GetFileName method:

Syntax
Object.GetFileName (Path)

Figure 3.28 – GetFileName Method Syntax Details

Argument	Description

Skype: rex.jones34
Twitter: @RexJonesII
Email: Rex.Jones@Test4Success.org
LinkedIn: https://www.linkedin.com/in/rexjones34

Object	Name of a FileSystemObject.
Path	The path to a specific file.

GetFileVersion

A GetFileVersion method returns the version number of the file in the specified path. The following is the syntax for GetFileVersion method:

Syntax
Object.GetFileVersion (Path)

Figure 3.29 – GetFileVersion Method Syntax Details

Argument	Description
Object	Name of a FileSystemObject.
Path	The path to a specific file.

GetFolder

A GetFolder method returns a Folder object corresponding to the folder in a specified path. The following is the syntax for GetFolder method:

Syntax
Object.GetFolder (Folder)

Figure 3.30 – GetFolder Method Syntax Details

Argument	Description
Object	Name of a FileSystemObject.
Folder	The path to a specific folder.

GetParentFolderName

A GetParentFolderName method returns the parent folder name of the last file or folder in a specified path. The following is the syntax for GetParentFolderName method:

3 Tips To Master QTP/UFT Within 30 Days
http://tinyurl.com/3-Tips-For-QTP-UFT

Free Webinars, Videos, and Live Trainings
http://tinyurl.com/Free-QTP-UFT-Selenium

Syntax
Object.GetParentFolderName (Path)

Figure 3.31 – GetParentFolderName Method Syntax Details

Argument	Description
Object	Name of a FileSystemObject.
Path	The path whose parent folder name will be returned.

GetSpecialFolder

A GetSpecialFolder method returns the path to a special folder (\Windows, \System, or \TMP). The following is the syntax for GetSpecialFolder method:

Syntax
Object.GetSpecialFolder (Folder)

Figure 3.32 – GetSpecialFolder Method Syntax Details

Argument	Description
Object	Name of a FileSystemObject.
Folder	The special folder name that will be returned. Can be one of the following constants/values: WindowsFolder / 0: A folder consisting of files installed by the Windows Operating System. SystemFolder / 1: A folder consisting of libraries, fonts, and device drivers. TemporaryFolder / 2: A folder used to store temporary files found in the TMP environment variable.

GetStandardStream

A GetStandardStream method returns a TextStream object corresponding to the standard input, output, or error stream. The following is the syntax for GetStandardStream method:

Syntax
Object.GetStandardStream (StandardStreamType [, Unicode])

Figure 3.33 – GetStandardStream Method Syntax Details

Argument	Description
Object	Name of a FileSystemObject.
StandardStreamType	Can be one of the following constants/values: StdIn / 0: Returns a TextStream object for the standard input stream. StdOut / 1: Returns a TextStream object for the standard output stream. StdErr / 2: Returns a TextStream object for the standard error stream.
Unicode	Boolean value that specifies if the file is created as Unicode or ASCII. The default file is ASCII. True: Indicates the file is created as Unicode. False: Indicates the file is created as ASCII.

GetTempName

A GetTempName method returns a random generated file name or folder name for a temporary file or folder. The following is the syntax for GetTempName method:

Syntax
Object.GetTempName ()

Figure 3.34 – GetTempName Method Syntax Details

Argument	Description
Object	Name of a FileSystemObject.

Move

A Move method moves the specified file or folder from one location (source) to another location (destination). The following is the syntax for Move method:

Syntax
Object.Move (Destination)

3 Tips To Master QTP/UFT Within 30 Days
http://tinyurl.com/3-Tips-For-QTP-UFT

Free Webinars, Videos, and Live Trainings
http://tinyurl.com/Free-QTP-UFT-Selenium

Figure 3.35 – Move Method Syntax Details

Argument	Description
Object	Name of a File or Folder object.
Destination	The path where the file(s) or folder(s) are to be moved which cannot include wildcard characters.

MoveFile

A MoveFile method moves one or more files from one location (source) to another location (destination). The following is the syntax for MoveFile method:

Syntax

Object.MoveFile (Source, Destination)

Figure 3.36 – MoveFile Method Syntax Details

Argument	Description
Object	Name of a FileSystemObject.
Source	The path of the file(s) to be moved which can include wildcard characters.
Destination	The path where the file(s) are to be moved which cannot include wildcard characters.

MoveFolder

A MoveFolder method moves one or more folders from one location (source) to another location (destination). The following is the syntax for MoveFolder method:

Syntax

Object.MoveFolder (Source, Destination)

Figure 3.37 – MoveFolder Method Syntax Details

Argument	Description
Object	Name of a FileSystemObject.

Skype: rex.jones34
Twitter: @RexJonesII
Email: Rex.Jones@Test4Success.org
LinkedIn: https://www.linkedin.com/in/rexjones34

| Source | The path of the folder(s) to be moved which can include wildcard characters. |
| Destination | The path where the folder(s) are to be moved which cannot include wildcard characters. |

OpenAsTextStream

An OpenAsTextStream method opens the specified file and returns a TextStream object that can be used to read from a file, write to a file, or attach to a file. The following is the syntax for OpenAsTextStream method:

Syntax
Object.OpenAsTextStream ([IOMode, [Format]])

Figure 3.38 – OpenAsTextStream Method Syntax Details

Argument	Description
Object	Name of a File object.
IOMode	The Input/Output Mode can be one of the following constants/values: ForReading / 1: Open a file for reading only. ForWriting / 2: Open a file for writing only. ForAppending / 8: Open a file and write to the end of the file.
Format	Tristate values are used to determine the format of the opened file. Can be one of the following constants/values: TristateTrue / -1: Open the file as Unicode TristateFalse / 0: Open the file as ASCII "Default = ASCII" TristateUseDefault / -2: Open the file as system default

OpenTextFile

An OpenTextFile method opens the specified file and returns a TextStream object that can be used to read from a file, write to a file, or attach to a file. The following is the syntax for OpenTextFile method:

3 Tips To Master QTP/UFT Within 30 Days
http://tinyurl.com/3-Tips-For-QTP-UFT

Free Webinars, Videos, and Live Trainings
http://tinyurl.com/Free-QTP-UFT-Selenium

Syntax

Object.OpenTextFile (FileName [, IOMode [, Create [, Format]]])

Figure 3.39 – OpenTextFile Method Syntax Details

Argument	Description
Object	Name of a FileSystemObject.
FileName	The string that determines the file to open.
IOMode	The Input/Output Mode can be one of the following constants/values: ForReading / 1: Open a file for reading only. ForWriting / 2: Open a file for writing only. ForAppending / 8: Open a file and write to the end of the file.
Create	Boolean value specifies if a new file will be created if the filename does not exist. The default it False. True: Indicates the specified file will be created. False: Indicates the specified file will not be created.
Format	Tristate values are used to determine the format of the opened file. Can be one of the following constants/values: TristateTrue / -1: Open the file as Unicode TristateFalse / 0: Open the file as ASCII "Default = ASCII" TristateUseDefault / -2: Open the file as system default

Read

A Read method reads a specific amount of characters from a TextStream file and returns the string. The following is the syntax for Read method:

Syntax

Object.Read (Characters)

Figure 3.40 – Read Method Syntax Details

Argument	Description
Object	Name of a TextStream object.
Characters	Number of characters read from a file.

Skype: rex.jones34
Twitter: @RexJonesII
Email: Rex.Jones@Test4Success.org
LinkedIn: https://www.linkedin.com/in/rexjones34

ReadAll

A ReadAll method reads the whole TextStream file and returns the string. The following is the syntax for ReadAll method:

Syntax
Object.ReadAll ()

Figure 3.41 – ReadAll Method Syntax Details

Argument	Description
Object	Name of a TextStream object.

ReadLine

A ReadLine method reads an entire line from a TextStream file and returns the string. The following is the syntax for ReadLine method:

Syntax
Object.ReadLine ()

Figure 3.42 – ReadLine Method Syntax Details

Argument	Description
Object	Name of a TextStream object.

Skip

A Skip method skips a specific amount of characters when reading a TextStream file. The following is the syntax for Skip method:

Syntax
Object.Skip (Characters)

Figure 3.43 – Skip Method Syntax Details

Argument	Description
Object	Name of a TextStream object.
Characters	Number of characters skipped when reading a file.

SkipLine

A SkipLine method skips the next line when reading a TextStream file. The following is the syntax for SkipLine method:

Syntax
Object.SkipLine ()

Figure 3.44 – SkipLine Method Syntax Details

Argument	Description
Object	Name of a TextStream object.

Write

A Write method writes the specified string to a TextStream file. The following is the syntax for Write method:

Syntax
Object.Write (String)

Figure 3.45 – Write Method Syntax Details

Argument	Description
Object	Name of a TextStream object.
String	The data written to a file.

Skype: rex.jones34
Twitter: @RexJonesII
Email: Rex.Jones@Test4Success.org
LinkedIn: https://www.linkedin.com/in/rexjones34

WriteBlankLines

A WriteBlankLines method writes a specified amount of newline characters to a TextStream file. The following is the syntax for WriteBlankLines method:

Syntax
Object.WriteBlankLines (Lines)

Figure 3.46 – WriteBlankLines Method Syntax Details

Argument	Description
Object	Name of a TextStream object.
Lines	The number of newline characters written to a file.

WriteLine

A WriteLine method writes a specific string and newline characters to a TextStream file. The following is the syntax for WriteLine method:

Syntax
Object.WriteLine ([String])

Figure 3.47 – WriteLine Method Syntax Details

Argument	Description
Object	Name of a TextStream object.
String	The data written to a file. A newline character is written to the file if no data is written.

Properties

The following is a list of properties in alphabetical order for all FSO objects and collections. Some of the properties are applicable to multiple objects and/or collections:

3 Tips To Master QTP/UFT Within 30 Days.
http://tinyurl.com/3-Tips-For-QTP-UFT

Free Webinars, Videos, and Live Trainings
http://tinyurl.com/Free-QTP-UFT-Selenium

Figure 3.48 – List of Objects and Collections

Object	Collections
Drive	Drives
File	Files
FileSystemObject	Folders
Folder	
TextStream	

The explanation of each property briefly states its associated object and/or collection along with its syntax:

Figure 3.49 – List of Properties

AtEndOfLine	IsRootFolder
AtEndOfStream	Item
Attributes	Key
AvailableSpace	Line
Column	Name
Count	ParentFolder
DateCreated	Path
DateLastAccessed	RootFolder
DateLastModified	SerialNumber
Drive	ShareName
DriveLetter	ShortName
Drives	ShortPath
DriveType	Size
Files	SubFolders
FileSystem	TotalSize
FreeSpace	Type
IsReady	VolumeName

Skype: rex.jones34
Twitter: @RexJonesII
Email: Rex.Jones@Test4Success.org
LinkedIn: https://www.linkedin.com/in/rexjones34

AtEndOfLine

An AtEndOfLine property returns a Boolean value. True if the file pointer is positioned immediately before the file's end-of-line marker in a TextStream file while False if it is not before the file's end-of-line marker. An error occurs if the specified file is not open for reading. The following is the syntax for AtEndOfLine property:

Syntax
Object.AtEndOfLine

Figure 3.50 – AtEndOfLine Property Syntax Details

Argument	Description
Object	Name of a TextStream object.

AtEndOfStream

An AtEndOfStream property returns a Boolean value. True if the file pointer is positioned at the end of a file while False if not at the end of a file. An error occurs if the specified file is not open for reading. The following is the syntax for AtEndOfStream property:

Syntax
Object.AtEndOfStream

Figure 3.51 – AtEndOfStream Property Syntax Details

Argument	Description
Object	Name of a TextStream object.

Attributes

An Attributes property sets or returns the attributes of files or folders. The following is the syntax for Attributes property:

Syntax
Object.Attributes [= NewAttributes]

3 Tips To Master QTP/UFT Within 30 Days
http://tinyurl.com/3-Tips-For-QTP-UFT

Free Webinars, Videos, and Live Trainings
http://tinyurl.com/Free-QTP-UFT-Selenium

Figure 3.52 – Attributes Property Syntax Details

Argument	Description
Object	Name of a File or Folder object.
NewAttributes	The new value for the attributes of the specified object.

The following is a list of values for the NewAttributes Argument:

Figure 3.53 – NewAttribute Argument Values

Argument	Value	Description	Read/Write
Normal	0	Normal file.	Attributes are not set.
ReadOnly	1	Read-only file.	Attribute is read/write.
Hidden	2	Hidden file.	Attribute is read/write.
System	4	System file.	Attribute is read/write.
Volume	8	Disk drive volume label.	Attribute is read-only.
Directory	16	Folder or directory.	Attribute is read-only.
Archive	32	File has changed since last backup.	Attribute is read/write.
Alias	1024	Link or shortcut.	Attribute is read-only.
Compressed	2048	Compressed file.	Attribute is read-only.

AvailableSpace

An AvailableSpace property returns the amount of space available on a drive or network share. The following is the syntax for AvailableSpace property:

Syntax
Object.AvailableSpace

Figure 3.54 – AvailableSpace Property Syntax Details

Argument	Description
Object	Name of a Drive object.

Column

A Column property returns the column number of the current character position in a TextStream file. The following is the syntax for Column property:

Syntax
Object.Column

Figure 3.55 – Column Property Syntax Details

Argument	Description
Object	Name of a TextStream object.

Count

A Count property returns the number of items in a collection or Dictionary object. The following is the syntax for Count property:

Syntax
Object.Count

Figure 3.56 – Count Property Syntax Details

Argument	Description
Object	Name of a Dictionary object, Drives collection, Files collection, or Folders collection.

DateCreated

A DateCreated property returns the creation date and time of the specified file or folder. The following is the syntax for DateCreated property:

Syntax
Object.DateCreated

Figure 3.57 – DateCreated Property Syntax Details

Argument	Description

3 Tips To Master QTP/UFT Within 30 Days
http://tinyurl.com/3-Tips-For-QTP-UFT

Free Webinars, Videos, and Live Trainings
http://tinyurl.com/Free-QTP-UFT-Selenium

Object	Name of a File or Folder object.

DateLastAccessed

A DateLastAccessed property returns the last accessed date and time of the specified file or folder. The following is the syntax for DateLastAccessed property:

Syntax
Object.DateLastAccessed

Figure 3.58 – DateLastAccessed Property Syntax Details

Argument	Description
Object	Name of a File or Folder object.

DateLastModified

A DateLastModified property returns the last modified date and time of the specified file or folder. The following is the syntax for DateLastModified property:

Syntax
Object.DateLastModified

Figure 3.59 – DateLastModified Property Syntax Details

Argument	Description
Object	Name of a File or Folder object.

Drive

A Drive property returns the drive letter of the drive where the specified file or folder resides. The following is the syntax for Drive property:

Syntax
Object.Drive

Figure 3.60 – Drive Property Syntax Details

Argument	Description

Skype: rex.jones34
Twitter: @RexJonesII
Email: Rex.Jones@Test4Success.org
LinkedIn: https://www.linkedin.com/in/rexjones34

| Object | Name of a File or Folder object. |

DriveLetter

A DriveLetter property returns the drive letter of a physical local drive or network share. The following is the syntax for DriveLetter property:

Syntax
Object.DriveLetter

Figure 3.61 – DriveLetter Property Syntax Details

Argument	Description
Object	Name of a Drive object.

Drives

A Drives property returns a Drives collection consisting of all the Drive objects on a local computer. The following is the syntax for Drives property:

Syntax
Object.Drives

Figure 3.62 - Drives Property Syntax Details

Argument	Description
Object	Name of a FileSystemObject.

DriveType

A DriveType property returns an integer indicating a specified drive type. The following is the syntax for DriveType property:

Syntax
Object.DriveType

Figure 3.63 – DriveType Property Syntax Details

Argument	Description
Object	Name of a Drive object.

Files

A Files property returns a Files collection comprised of all File objects included in the specified folder. The following is the syntax for Files property:

Syntax
Object.Files

Figure 3.64 – Files Property Syntax Details

Argument	Description
Object	Name of a Folder object.

FileSystem

A FileSystem property returns the file system type for the specified drive. The following is the syntax for FileSystem property:

Syntax
Object.FileSystem

Figure 3.65 – FileSystem Property Syntax Details

Argument	Description
Object	Name of a Drive object.

FreeSpace

A FreeSpace property returns the available free space on the specified drive or network share. The following is the syntax for FreeSpace property:

Syntax
Object.FreeSpace

Skype: rex.jones34
Twitter: @RexJonesII
Email: Rex.Jones@Test4Success.org
LinkedIn: https://www.linkedin.com/in/rexjones34

Chapter 3
FileSystemObject (FSO)   You Must Learn VBScript for QTP/UFT

Figure 3.66 – FreeSpace Property Syntax Details

Argument	Description
Object	Name of a Drive object.

IsReady

An IsReady property returns a Boolean value. True if the specified drive is ready and False if the specified drive is not ready. The following is the syntax for IsReady property:

Syntax
Object.IsReady

Figure 3.67 – IsReady Property Syntax Details

Argument	Description
Object	Name of a Drive object.

IsRootFolder

An IsRootFolder returns a Boolean value. True if the specified folder is the root folder and False if the specified folder is not the root folder. The following is the syntax for IsRootFolder property:

Syntax
Object.IsRootFolder

Figure 3.68 – IsRootFolder Property Syntax Details

Argument	Description
Object	Name of a Folder object.

Item

An Item property sets or returns the value of an item in the collection denoted by a specified key. The following is the syntax for Item property:

3 Tips To Master QTP/UFT Within 30 Days
http://tinyurl.com/3-Tips-For-QTP-UFT

Free Webinars, Videos, and Live Trainings
http://tinyurl.com/Free-QTP-UFT-Selenium

Syntax
Object.Item (Key) [= NewItem]

Figure 3.69 – Item Property Syntax Details

Argument	Description
Object	Name of an FSO collection or Dictionary object.
Key	Associated with the item getting returned or added.
NewItem	Only used for Dictionary object. New value for the specified key.

Key

A Key property changes the value of an existing key in a Dictionary object. The following is the syntax for Key property:

Syntax
Object.Key(ExistingKey) = NewKey

Figure 3.70 – Key Property Syntax Details

Argument	Description
Object	Name of a Dictionary object.
ExistingKey	Value of existing key.
NewKey	New key value that replaces the existing key. If an existing key is not located then a new key is created with an associated empty item.

Line

A Line property returns the current line number in a TextStream file. The following is the syntax for Line property:

Syntax
Object.Line

Figure 3.71 – Line Property Syntax Details

Argument	Description
Object	Name of a TextStream object.

Skype: rex.jones34
Twitter: @RexJonesII
Email: Rex.Jones@Test4Success.org
LinkedIn: https://www.linkedin.com/in/rexjones34

Name

A Name property sets or returns the specified file name or folder name. The following is the syntax for Name property:

Syntax
Object.Name [= NewName]

Figure 3.72 – Name Property Syntax Details

Argument	Description
Object	Name of a File or Folder object.
NewName	New name of the specified object.

ParentFolder

A ParentFolder property returns the parent Folder object of the specified file or folder. The following is the syntax for ParentFolder property:

Syntax
Object.ParentFolder

Figure 3.73 – ParentFolder Property Syntax Details

Argument	Description
Object	Name of a File or Folder object.

Path

A Path property returns the path for a specified file, folder, or object. The following is the syntax for Path property:

Syntax
Object.Path

Figure 3.74 – Path Property Syntax Details

Argument	Description

3 Tips To Master QTP/UFT Within 30 Days
http://tinyurl.com/3-Tips-For-QTP-UFT

Free Webinars, Videos, and Live Trainings
http://tinyurl.com/Free-QTP-UFT-Selenium

Object	Name of a <u>File</u>, <u>Folder</u> or <u>Drive</u> object.

RootFolder

A RootFolder property returns a Folder object that serves as the root folder of a specified drive. The following is the syntax for RootFolder property:

Syntax
Object.RootFolder

Figure 3.75 – RootFolder Property Syntax Details

Argument	Description
Object	Name of a <u>Drive</u> object.

SerialNumber

A SerialNumber property returns the decimal serial number used to determine a disk volume. The following is the syntax for SerialNumber property:

Syntax
Object.SerialNumber

Figure 3.76 – SerialNumber Property Syntax Details

Argument	Description
Object	Name of a <u>Drive</u> object.

ShareName

A ShareName property returns the network share name in Universal Naming Convention (UNC) for a specified drive. The following is the syntax for ShareName property:

Syntax
Object.ShareName

Figure 3.77 – ShareName Property Syntax Details

Argument	Description

Object	Name of a Drive object.

ShortName

A ShortName property returns the short version of a folder name. The following is the syntax for ShortName property:

Syntax
Object.ShortName

Figure 3.78 – ShortName Property Syntax Details

Argument	Description
Object	Name of a File or Folder object.

ShortPath

A ShortPath property returns the short version of a folder path. The following is the syntax for ShortPath property:

Syntax
Object.ShortPath

Figure 3.79 – ShortPath Property Syntax Details

Argument	Description
Object	Name of a File or Folder object.

Size

A Size property returns the size of the specified file or folder. Files return the size in bytes for a specified file while folders returns the size in bytes for all files and subfolders in the folder. The following is the syntax for Size property:

Syntax
Object.Size

Figure 3.80 – Size Property Syntax Details

Argument	Description
Object	Name of a File or Folder object.

SubFolders

A SubFolders property returns a Folders collection comprised of all folders contained in the specified folder. The following is the syntax for SubFolders property:

Figure 3.81 – SubFolders Property Syntax Details

Argument	Description
Object	Name of a Folder object.

TotalSize

A TotalSize property returns the total space in bytes of the specified drive or network share. The following is the syntax for TotalSize property:

Syntax
Object.TotalSize

Figure 3.82 – TotalSize Property Syntax Details

Argument	Description
Object	Name of a Drive object.

Type

A Type property returns information about the file type or folder type. The following is the syntax for Type property:

Syntax
Object.Type

Figure 3.83 – Type Property Syntax Details

Argument	Description
Object	Name of a File or Folder object.

VolumeName

A VolumeName property sets or returns the volume name of the specified drive. The following is the syntax for VolumeName property:

Syntax
Object.VolumeName [= NewName]

Figure 3.84 – VolumeName Property Syntax Details

Argument	Description
Object	Name of a Drive object.
NewName	New name of the specified object.

Chapter 3 discussed files, folders, and drives regarding the FileSystemObject (FSO). FSO has five objects and three collections. The five objects are Drive, File, FileSystemObject, Folder, and TextStream while the three collections are Drives, Files, and Folders. Information associated to the computer system can be created, retrieved, or located. Chapter 4 explains classes, which serve as a template for objects.

Chapter 4
Classes

Classes serve as containers for objects. A class is the block of code that is created at design time, as opposed to an object that uses code at run time. An object stores data in the form of properties and performs actions by way of methods. Thousands of objects can be established after creating a class.

Chapter 4 explains the following regarding Classes:

- ✓ Class Statement
- ✓ Class Properties
- ✓ Class Methods
- ✓ Class Events

Class Statement

The key to forming a class is the Class statement. Class statements utilize the Class and the End Class blocks as boundaries for a class. The following is the syntax for a Class statement.

Syntax
Class NameOfClass()
   code
End Class

Figure 4.1 – Class Statement Syntax Details

Argument	Description
NameOfClass	Name of the class which must not be the same as any VBScript reserved word.

Skype: rex.jones34
Twitter: @RexJonesII
Email: Rex.Jones@Test4Success.org
LinkedIn: https://www.linkedin.com/in/rexjones34

Chapter 4
Classes   You Must Learn VBScript for QTP/UFT

Code	One or more lines of code that define variables, properties, and methods of a class.

The following screenshot shows the Mercury Tours Flight Finder page:

Figure 4.2 – Mercury Tours Flight Finder Page

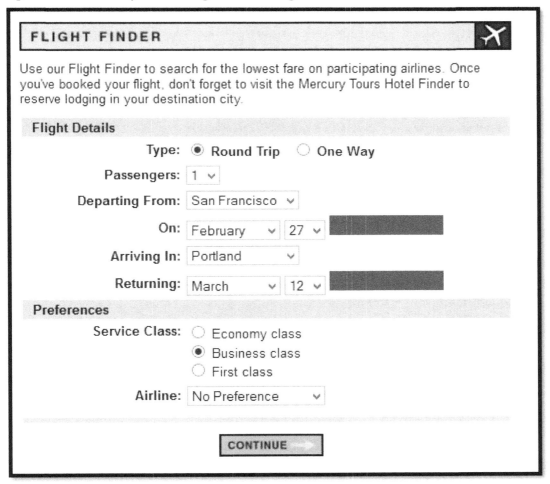

The following is a Class statement example which includes the Mercury Tours Flight Finder page as an object:

Figure 4.3 – Screenshot of Sample Code

```vbscript
1    Option Explicit
2
3    Dim MERCURYTOURS_SETUP
4    Dim brMercuryTours
5    Dim pgHome, pgFlightFinder, pgSelectFlight, pgBookFlight, pgFlightConfirmation
6
7    Set MERCURYTOURS_SETUP = New class_SetupTearDown
8
9    Class class_SetupTearDown
10       Sub Class_Initialize()
11
12           Set brMercuryTours = Browser("Welcome: Mercury Tours")
13           Set pgHome = brMercuryTours.Page("Welcome: Mercury Tours")
14           Set pgFlightFinder = brMercuryTours.Page("Find a Flight: Mercury")
15           Set pgSelectFlight = brMercuryTours.Page("Select a Flight: Mercury")
16           Set pgBookFlight = brMercuryTours.Page("Book a Flight: Mercury")
17           Set pgFlightConfirmation = brMercuryTours.Page("Flight Confirmation: Mercury")
18
19       End Sub
20
21       Sub Class_Terminate()
22
23           Set brMercuryTours = Nothing
24           Set pgHome = Nothing
25           Set pgFlightFinder = Nothing
26           Set pgSelectFlight = Nothing
27           Set pgBookFlight = Nothing
28           Set pgFlightConfirmation = Nothing
29
30       End Sub
31   End Class
```

Option Explicit

Dim MERCURYTOURS_SETUP
Dim brMercuryTours

Skype: rex.jones34
Twitter: @RexJonesII
Email: Rex.Jones@Test4Success.org
LinkedIn: https://www.linkedin.com/in/rexjones34

Chapter 4
Classes   You Must Learn VBScript for QTP/UFT

```
Dim pgHome, pgFlightFinder, pgSelectFlight, pgBookFlight, pgFlightConfirmation

Set MERCURYTOURS_SETUP = New class_SetupTearDown

Class class_SetupTearDown
  Sub Class_Initialize()

    Set brMercuryTours = Browser("Welcome: Mercury Tours")
    Set pgHome = brMercuryTours.Page("Welcome: Mercury Tours")
    Set pgFlightFinder = brMercuryTours.Page("Find a Flight: Mercury")
    Set pgSelectFlight = brMercuryTours.Page("Select a Flight: Mercury")
    Set pgBookFlight = brMercuryTours.Page("Book a Flight: Mercury")
       Set pgFlightConfirmation = brMercuryTours.Page("Flight Confirmation:
Mercury")

  End Sub

  Sub Class_Terminate()

    Set brMercuryTours = Nothing
    Set pgHome = Nothing
    Set pgFlightFinder = Nothing
    Set pgSelectFlight = Nothing
    Set pgBookFlight = Nothing
    Set pgFlightConfirmation = Nothing

  End Sub
End Class
```

Members such as variables "pgHome" and methods "Sub Function" are declared within the Class statement. All members of a class may be declared as Public or Private.

3 Tips To Master QTP/UFT Within 30 Days
http://tinyurl.com/3-Tips-For-QTP-UFT

Free Webinars, Videos, and Live Trainings
http://tinyurl.com/Free-QTP-UFT-Selenium

Class Properties

Class properties are the structures through which data is stored and accessed whenever a script creates an object within a class. The data can be stored in an object or returned from the object via a property. Properties are one of the following two types:

1. Private Property
2. Public Property

Private Property

A Private property contains information that is not accessible by code outside of a class. Information can be in the form of variables or code. Variables defined at the class level and declared with a Private statement are called private property variables. Private property variables contain the value of the following properties:

1. Property Let
2. Property Get
3. Property Set

Property Let

A Property Let procedure allows code outside of a class to set a value in a private property variable, but does not return a value. It is beneficial for this property to accept at least one argument. If at least one argument is not accepted, then the Property Let procedure holds no value in allowing outside code to store a value in the private property variable. The following is the syntax for the Property Let procedure:

Syntax
[Public | Private] Property Let ProcedureName ([ArgList,] Value)
  [Code]
  [Exit Property]
  [Code]
End Property

Skype: rex.jones34
Twitter: @RexJonesII
Email: Rex.Jones@Test4Success.org
LinkedIn: https://www.linkedin.com/in/rexjones34

Figure 4.4 – Property Let Syntax Details

Argument	Description
Public	The default statement that allows the procedure to be accessed by outside code.
Private	Allows access to other procedures in the same class.
ProcedureName	Name of the procedure.
ArgList	List of variables characterizing the arguments passed to the procedure.
Value	Variable that contains the value assigned to the property.
Code	A line or group of lines executed by the procedure.
Exit Property	Force an immediate exit from the procedure.

The following example utilizes the Property Let procedure:

Figure 4.5 – Screenshot of Sample Code

```
1    Option Explicit
2
3  ⊟ Class FlightFinder
4
5        Private cl_strDepartFrom
6
7  ⊟      Public Property Let FlightDetails (strDepartFrom)
8              cl_strDepartFrom = strDepartFrom
9           End Property
10
11  └ End Class
```

Option Explicit

Class FlightFinder

  Private cl_strDepartFrom

3 Tips To Master QTP/UFT Within 30 Days
http://tinyurl.com/3-Tips-For-QTP-UFT

Free Webinars, Videos, and Live Trainings
http://tinyurl.com/Free-QTP-UFT-Selenium

> **Public Property Let** FlightDetails (strDepartFrom)
>   cl_strDepartFrom = strDepartFrom
> **End Property**

End Class

The code inside of the Property Let procedure stores the value from "strDepartFrom" into the procedure's private property variable "cl_strDepartFrom."

Property Get

A Property Get procedure allows code outside of a class to read the value of a private property variable and return a value to the calling code. An argument can be added to this property. If an argument is added, an extra argument must be added to the Property Let and Property Set procedures. The Property Get procedure must always possess one less argument than the Property Let and Property Set procedures. The following is the syntax for the Property Get procedure:

Syntax
[Public | Private] Property Get ProcedureName [(Arglist)]
   [Code]
   [**[Set]** ProcedureName = Expression]
   [**Exit Property**]
   [Code]
   [**[Set]** ProcedureName = Expression]
End Property

Figure 4.6 – Property Get Syntax Details

Argument	Description
Public	The default statement that allows the procedure to be accessed by outside code.
Private	Allows access to other procedures in the same class.
ProcedureName	Name of the procedure.

Skype: rex.jones34
Twitter: @RexJonesII
Email: Rex.Jones@Test4Success.org
LinkedIn: https://www.linkedin.com/in/rexjones34

ArgList	List of variables characterizing the arguments passed to the procedure.
Code	A line or group of lines executed by the procedure.
Set	Keyword that is used to assign an object as the return value.
Expression	Return value of the procedure if keyword Set is provided.
Exit Property	Force an immediate exit from the procedure.

Figure 4.7 – Screenshot of Sample Code

```
1    Option Explicit
2
3  ⊟ Class FlightFinder
4
5        Private cl_strDepartFrom
6
7  ⊟      Public Property Let FlightDetails (strDepartFrom)
8              cl_strDepartFrom = strDepartFrom
9  └      End Property
10
11 ⊟      Public Property Get FlightDetails ()
12              Set FlightDetails = cl_strDepartFrom
13 └      End Property
14
15 └End Class
```

Option Explicit

Class FlightFinder

   Private cl_strDepartFrom

   Public Property Let FlightDetails (strDepartFrom)
    cl_strDepartFrom = strDepartFrom
   End Property

3 Tips To Master QTP/UFT Within 30 Days
http://tinyurl.com/3-Tips-For-QTP-UFT

Free Webinars, Videos, and Live Trainings
http://tinyurl.com/Free-QTP-UFT-Selenium

Public Property Get FlightDetails ()
   Set FlightDetails = cl_strDepartFrom
End Property

End Class

- o The Property Let procedure stores a value in the private property variable "cl_strDepartFrom"
- o The Property Get procedure reads the value of the private property variable "cl_strDepartFrom"

Property Set

A Property Set procedure allows code outside of a class to set a value in a private property variable, but does not return a value. The Property Set and Property Let procedures are similar in functionality. However, the Property Set procedure is reserved for objects rather than variables. In addition, code outside of the class must use the Set Object.Property = Object syntax to set a value in the private property variable. The following is the syntax for the Property Set procedure:

Syntax
[Public | Private] Property Set ProcedureName([ArgList,] Reference)
  [Code]
  [[**Set**] PrivatePropertyVariable = Reference]
  [**Exit Property**]
  [Code]
  [[**Set**] PrivatePropertyVariable = Reference]
End Property

Figure 4.8 – Property Set Syntax Details

Argument	Description

Public	The default statement that allows the procedure to be accessed by outside code.
Private	Allows access to other procedures in the same class.
ProcedureName	Name of the procedure.
ArgList	List of variables characterizing the arguments passed to the procedure.
Reference	Variable that contains the object reference on the right side of the object reference assignment.
Code	A line or group of lines executed by the procedure.
Set	Keyword that is used to assign an object as the return value.
PrivatePropertyVariable	Variable declared at the class level and defined with a Private statement if keyword Set is provided.
Exit Property	Force an immediate exit from the procedure.

The following example utilizes the Property Set procedure:

Figure 4.9 – Screenshot of Sample Code

```
1    Option Explicit
2
3  ⊟ Class FlightFinder
4
5        Private cl_objPassengers
6
7  ⊟      Public Property Set FlightDetails (objPassengers)
8             cl_objPassengers = objPassengers
9  ─      End Property
10
11 ⊟      Public Property Let FlightDetails (strPassengers)
12             Set cl_objPassengers = strPassengers
13 ─      End Property
14
15 └End Class
```

Option Explicit

Class FlightFinder

   Private cl_objPassengers

   Public Property Set FlightDetails (objPassengers)
     cl_objPassengers = objPassengers
   End Property

   Public Property Let FlightDetails (strPassengers)
     Set cl_objPassengers = strPassengers
   End Property

End Class

- o The Property Set procedure stores a value from the object reference "objPassengers" in the private property variable "cl_objPassengers "

Skype: rex.jones34
Twitter: @RexJonesII
Email: Rex.Jones@Test4Success.org
LinkedIn: https://www.linkedin.com/in/rexjones34

- o The Property Let procedure stores a value from the variable "strPassengers" in the private property variable "cl_objPassengers "

Note: All of the examples used the same procedure name "FlightDetails" for each property (see Figures 4.5, 4.7, and 4.9). It is not a requirement but procedures are allowed to have the same procedure name in the same class.

Read-Only/Write-Only Properties

Properties within a Class can be formed as read-only or write-only. A property can be made read-only and write-only one of two ways:

Read-Only Properties

The following are two ways to generate a read-only property:

1. Only implement a Property Get procedure for the property
2. Declare the Property Get procedure as Public and the Property Let procedure as Private

The following is an example of the first way:

Figure 4.10 – Screenshot of Sample Code utilizing Figure 4.2

```
1    Option Explicit
2
3   ⊟ Class FlightFinder
4
5        Private cl_strAirline
6
7   ⊟    Public Property Get AirlineName ()
8            AirlineName = cl_strAirline
9        End Property
10
11   └ End Class
```

Option Explicit

Class FlightFinder

   Private cl_strAirline

   Public Property Get AirlineName ()
     AirlineName = cl_strAirline
   End Property

End Class

Code outside of the class "FlightFinder" cannot write to the Property Get property "AirlineName." The following is an example of the second way:

Figure 4.11 – Screenshot of Sample Code utilizing Figure 4.2

```
1    Option Explicit
2
3   Class FlightFinder
4
5        Private cl_strAirline
6
7        Private Property Let AirlineName(strAirline)
8            cl_strAirline = strAirline
9        End Property
10
11        Public Property Get AirlineName ()
12            AirlineName = cl_strAirline
13        End Property
14
15   End Class
```

Option Explicit

Class FlightFinder

Skype: rex.jones34
Twitter: @RexJonesII
Email: Rex.Jones@Test4Success.org
LinkedIn: https://www.linkedin.com/in/rexjones34

```
    Private cl_strAirline

    Private Property Let AirlineName(strAirline)
       cl_strAirline = strAirline
    End Property

    Public Property Get AirlineName ()
       AirlineName = cl_strAirline
    End Property
```

End Class

The Property Let procedure is declared as Private. Therefore, the property is hidden from code outside of the class. Code inside of the class can write to the property via the Property Let procedure.

Write-Only Properties
The following are two ways to generate a write-only property:

1. Only implement a Property Let procedure for the property
2. Declare the Property Let procedure as Public and the Property Get procedure as Private

Note: Both write-only ways are the opposite of their respective read-only counterpart.

Public Property
A Public property can be established for a class by not providing Property Let, Property Get, or Property Set procedures. In addition, all of the procedures can be declared with a Public statement. However, the following are the outcomes of Public Properties:

o   Outside code can write to all properties

3 Tips To Master QTP/UFT Within 30 Days
http://tinyurl.com/3-Tips-For-QTP-UFT

Free Webinars, Videos, and Live Trainings
http://tinyurl.com/Free-QTP-UFT-Selenium

- o Values that are written to a property cannot be validated without creating a Private Property Let procedure
- o Values that are read from a property cannot be validated without creating a Private Property Get procedure
- o Properties cannot be made read-only or write-only

Class Methods

A Class Method is another name for procedures (also known as functions) that is located in a class. There are two types of procedures which is Sub Procedure and Function Procedure. A Sub Procedure performs an action and takes arguments, but does not return a value. However, a Function Procedure performs an action, takes arguments, and returns a value. The main consideration is deciding to declare the method as Private or Public. Private statements are available to code inside of the class, while Public statements are available to code inside and outside of the class. The following is an example utilizing properties, methods, and code outside of a class:

Skype: rex.jones34
Twitter: @RexJonesII
Email: Rex.Jones@Test4Success.org
LinkedIn: https://www.linkedin.com/in/rexjones34

Figure 4.12 – Screenshot of Sample Code

```
1    Option Explicit
2
3  □ Class FlightFinder
4
5      Private cl_strServiceClass
6
7  □    Public Property Let GenerateServiceClass (strServiceClass)
8           cl_strServiceClass = strServiceClass
9        End Property
10
11 □    Public Sub DisplayServiceClass (strSvcClassInfo)
12          MsgBox ServiceClassOptions (strSvcClassInfo) & cl_strServiceClass
13        End Sub
14
15 □    Private Function ServiceClassOptions (strSvcClassInfo)
16          ServiceClassOptions = "The best available class is "
17        End Function
18
19  └End Class
20
21   Dim objGenerateClass
22
23   Set objGenerateClass = New FlightFinder
24
25   With objGenerateClass
26       .GenerateServiceClass = "Business class"
27       .DisplayServiceClass "Best"
28   End With
```

Option Explicit

Class FlightFinder

   Private cl_strServiceClass

   Public Property Let GenerateServiceClass (strServiceClass)

3 Tips To Master QTP/UFT Within 30 Days
http://tinyurl.com/3-Tips-For-QTP-UFT

Free Webinars, Videos, and Live Trainings
http://tinyurl.com/Free-QTP-UFT-Selenium

```
        cl_strServiceClass = strServiceClass
    End Property

    Public Sub DisplayServiceClass (strSvcClassInfo)
        MsgBox ServiceClassOptions (strSvcClassInfo) & cl_strServiceClass
    End Sub

    Private Function ServiceClassOptions (strSvcClassInfo)
        ServiceClassOptions = "The best available class is "
    End Function

End Class

Dim objGenerateClass

Set objGenerateClass = New FlightFinder

With objGenerateClass
    .GenerateServiceClass = "Business class"
    .DisplayServiceClass "Best"
End With
```

The output displays, "The best available class is Business class."

Figure 4.13 – Screenshot Displaying Output from Above Code

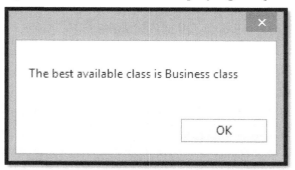

The following illustrates what is available to the outside code:

Figure 4.14 – Screenshot of Sample Code

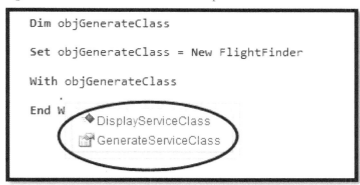

The Public property "GenerateServiceClass" and Public method "DisplayServiceClass" can be called by code outside of the class "FlightFinder". However, the Private property "ServiceClassOptions" is not available to outside code.

Class Events

Class events are special <u>methods</u> that are fired (also known as called) automatically. An automation engineer can choose to write an event handler that will be called whenever a class event fires. Event handlers have the ability to be attached to objects and allow execution of custom code. The custom code is executed automatically upon an event, such as loading a page, triggering that object. Event handlers are Sub Procedures that are optional in a given class. All classes provide a foundation for the following two types of class events:

1. <u>Class Initialize</u>
2. <u>Class Terminate</u>

Class Initialize

The Class Initialize event fires in a specific class when an object is instantiated (also known as created). The Class Initialize event is considered a constructor function that starts when the Sub Procedure is executed. However, the Class Initialize event does not accept arguments, but can perform actions like open a file or database connection. The following is the syntax for the Class Initialize event:

Syntax
Sub Class_Initialize ()
  Code
End Sub

Figure 4.15 – Class Initialize Event Syntax Details

Argument	Description
Class_Initialize	Name of the Sub Procedure to initialize. The name cannot be a different than Class_Initialize.
Code	Initializes the class and properties of the class

Skype: rex.jones34
Twitter: @RexJonesII
Email: Rex.Jones@Test4Success.org
LinkedIn: https://www.linkedin.com/in/rexjones34

The following example utilizes the Class Initialize event:

Figure 4.16 – Screenshot of Sample Code via Figure 4.3

```
1   Option Explicit
2
3   Dim MERCURYTOURS_SETUP
4   Dim brMercuryTours
5   Dim pgHome, pgFlightFinder, pgSelectFlight, pgBookFlight, pgFlightConfirmation
6
7   Set MERCURYTOURS_SETUP = New class_SetupTearDown
8
9   Class class_SetupTearDown
10      Sub Class_Initialize()
11
12          Set brMercuryTours = Browser("Welcome: Mercury Tours")
13          Set pgHome = brMercuryTours.Page("Welcome: Mercury Tours")
14          Set pgFlightFinder = brMercuryTours.Page("Find a Flight: Mercury")
15          Set pgSelectFlight = brMercuryTours.Page("Select a Flight: Mercury")
16          Set pgBookFlight = brMercuryTours.Page("Book a Flight: Mercury")
17          Set pgFlightConfirmation = brMercuryTours.Page("Flight Confirmation: Mercury")
18
19      End Sub
20
21      Sub Class_Terminate()
22
23          Set brMercuryTours = Nothing
24          Set pgHome = Nothing
25          Set pgFlightFinder = Nothing
26          Set pgSelectFlight = Nothing
27          Set pgBookFlight = Nothing
28          Set pgFlightConfirmation = Nothing
29
30      End Sub
31  End Class
```

Option Explicit

Dim MERCURYTOURS_SETUP

3 Tips To Master QTP/UFT Within 30 Days
http://tinyurl.com/3-Tips-For-QTP-UFT

Free Webinars, Videos, and Live Trainings
http://tinyurl.com/Free-QTP-UFT-Selenium

Dim brMercuryTours
Dim pgHome, pgFlightFinder, pgSelectFlight, pgBookFlight, pgFlightConfirmation

Set MERCURYTOURS_SETUP = **New** class_SetupTearDown

Class class_SetupTearDown
  Sub Class_Initialize()

    Set brMercuryTours = Browser("Welcome: Mercury Tours")
    Set pgHome = brMercuryTours.Page("Welcome: Mercury Tours")
    Set pgFlightFinder = brMercuryTours.Page("Find a Flight: Mercury")
    Set pgSelectFlight = brMercuryTours.Page("Select a Flight: Mercury")
    Set pgBookFlight = brMercuryTours.Page("Book a Flight: Mercury")
      Set pgFlightConfirmation = brMercuryTours.Page("Flight Confirmation: Mercury")

  End Sub

  Sub Class_Terminate()

    Set brMercuryTours = **Nothing**
    Set pgHome = **Nothing**
    Set pgFlightFinder = **Nothing**
    Set pgSelectFlight = **Nothing**
    Set pgBookFlight = **Nothing**
    Set pgFlightConfirmation = **Nothing**

  End Sub
End Class

The objects "brMercuryTours, pgHome, etc." are initialized and contain values when the class begins. As a result, if a page such as Browser("Welcome: Mercury Tours") loads, it will be assigned to object variable brMercuryTours.

Note: There can only be one Class_Initialize event in a class.

Class Terminate

The Class Terminate event fires in a specific class when an object is destroyed. The Class Terminate event is considered a destructor function that ends when the Sub Procedure is executed. However, the Class Terminate event does not accept arguments, but can perform actions like close a file or database connection. The following is the syntax for the Class Terminate event:

Syntax
Sub Class_Terminate ()
    Code
End Sub

Figure 4.17 – Class Initialize Event Syntax Details

Argument	Description
Class_Terminate	Name of the Sub Procedure to terminate. The name cannot be a different than Class_Terminate.
Code	Terminates the class and properties of the class

The following example utilizes the Class Terminate event:

3 Tips To Master QTP/UFT Within 30 Days
http://tinyurl.com/3-Tips-For-QTP-UFT

Free Webinars, Videos, and Live Trainings
http://tinyurl.com/Free-QTP-UFT-Selenium

Figure 4.18 – Screenshot of Sample Code via Figure 4.3

```
1    Option Explicit
2
3    Dim MERCURYTOURS_SETUP
4    Dim brMercuryTours
5    Dim pgHome, pgFlightFinder, pgSelectFlight, pgBookFlight, pgFlightConfirmation
6
7    Set MERCURYTOURS_SETUP = New class_SetupTearDown
8
9  ⊟ Class class_SetupTearDown
10 ⊟     Sub Class_Initialize()
11
12           Set brMercuryTours = Browser("Welcome: Mercury Tours")
13           Set pgHome = brMercuryTours.Page("Welcome: Mercury Tours")
14           Set pgFlightFinder = brMercuryTours.Page("Find a Flight: Mercury")
15           Set pgSelectFlight = brMercuryTours.Page("Select a Flight: Mercury")
16           Set pgBookFlight = brMercuryTours.Page("Book a Flight: Mercury")
17           Set pgFlightConfirmation = brMercuryTours.Page("Flight Confirmation: Mercury")
18
19       End Sub
20
21 ⊟     Sub Class_Terminate()
22
23           Set brMercuryTours = Nothing
24           Set pgHome = Nothing
25           Set pgFlightFinder = Nothing
26           Set pgSelectFlight = Nothing
27           Set pgBookFlight = Nothing
28           Set pgFlightConfirmation = Nothing
29
30       End Sub
31  End Class
```

Option Explicit

Dim MERCURYTOURS_SETUP
Dim brMercuryTours

Skype: rex.jones34
Twitter: @RexJonesII
Email: Rex.Jones@Test4Success.org
LinkedIn: https://www.linkedin.com/in/rexjones34

Dim pgHome, pgFlightFinder, pgSelectFlight, pgBookFlight, pgFlightConfirmation

Set MERCURYTOURS_SETUP = **New** class_SetupTearDown

Class class_SetupTearDown
  Sub Class_Initialize()

    Set brMercuryTours = Browser("Welcome: Mercury Tours")
    Set pgHome = brMercuryTours.Page("Welcome: Mercury Tours")
    Set pgFlightFinder = brMercuryTours.Page("Find a Flight: Mercury")
    Set pgSelectFlight = brMercuryTours.Page("Select a Flight: Mercury")
    Set pgBookFlight = brMercuryTours.Page("Book a Flight: Mercury")
    Set pgFlightConfirmation = brMercuryTours.Page("Flight Confirmation: Mercury")

  End Sub

  Sub Class_Terminate()

    Set brMercuryTours = **Nothing**
    Set pgHome = **Nothing**
    Set pgFlightFinder = **Nothing**
    Set pgSelectFlight = **Nothing**
    Set pgBookFlight = **Nothing**
    Set pgFlightConfirmation = **Nothing**

  End Sub
End Class

The objects "pgFlightFinder, pgSelectFlight, etc." are destroyed and contain no values when the class ends. An object can be destroyed in the following two ways:

3 Tips To Master QTP/UFT Within 30 Days
http://tinyurl.com/3-Tips-For-QTP-UFT

Free Webinars, Videos, and Live Trainings
http://tinyurl.com/Free-QTP-UFT-Selenium

1. When the object is explicitly assigned the value of Nothing
2. When the object variable with a reference to the object goes out of scope

Note: There can only be one Class_Terminate event in a class.

Chapter 4 covered classes which is a block of code created at design time and surrounded by the statements Class and End Class. A class has the potential to include thousands of objects, along with properties, methods, and events. Chapter 5 dives into regular expressions which are tools for searching and replacing patterns.

Chapter 5
Regular Expressions

Regular expressions are powerful tools for searching and/or replacing patterns. Prior to regular expressions, an automation engineer wrote several lines of code containing loops, InStr, and Mid functions to search and replace data. Now, it is possible to significantly reduce the amount of code to perform the same task utilizing regular expressions. The following is an example of a regular expression used to reduce taxes to zero if a flight is booked with four passengers:

Figure 5.1 – Mercury Tours – Book A Flight

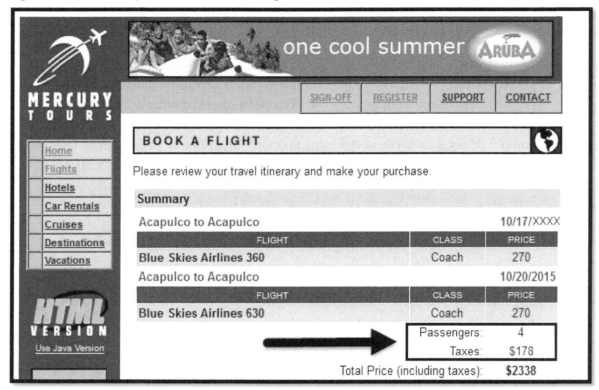

Chapter 5
Regular Expressions   You Must Learn VBScript for QTP/UFT

Figure 5.2 – Screenshot of Sample Code

```
1    Option Explicit
2
3    Dim curTaxes
4    Dim intPassengers
5    Dim objRegExp
6
7    Set objRegExp = New RegExp
8
9    objRegExp.Pattern = "\$.*"
10   intPassengers = 4
11
12   ' The value "$178" should get returned from the AUT via GetROProperty
13   ' rather than a hard-coded value. This is for demonstration purposes only
14   curTaxes = "$178"
15
16   MsgBox "The current Tax Amount is " & curTaxes
17   MsgBox "Special Promotion! " & vbCrlf & "Taxes get reduced to " & _
18   objRegExp.Replace (curTaxes, "$0") & " while having 4 passengers"
```

Option Explicit

Dim curTaxes
Dim intPassengers
Dim objRegExp

Set objRegExp = **New** RegExp

objRegExp.Pattern = "\$.*"
intPassengers = 4

' The value "$178" should get returned from the AUT via GetROProperty

3 Tips To Master QTP/UFT Within 30 Days
http://tinyurl.com/3-Tips-For-QTP-UFT

Free Webinars, Videos, and Live Trainings
http://tinyurl.com/Free-QTP-UFT-Selenium

' rather than a hard-coded value. This is for demonstration purposes only
curTaxes = "$178"

MsgBox "The current Tax Amount is " & curTaxes
MsgBox "Special Promotion! " & **vbCrlf** & "Taxes get reduced to " & _
objRegExp.**Replace** (curTaxes, "$0") & " while having 4 passengers"

- o   The first output displays "The current Tax Amount is $178"
- o   The second output displays "Special Promotion! / Taxes get reduced to $0 while having 4 passengers"

Figure 5.3 – Screenshots Displaying Output from Above Code

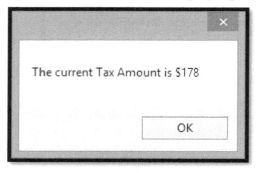

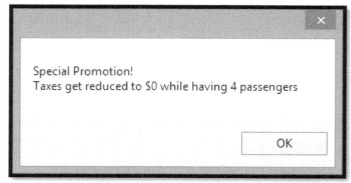

Skype: rex.jones34
Twitter: @RexJonesII
Email: Rex.Jones@Test4Success.org
LinkedIn: https://www.linkedin.com/in/rexjones34

The previous example is a regular expression that finds and replaces data. The seventh code line, "**Set** objRegExp = **New** RegExp," creates a new regular expression object. The ninth code line, "objRegExp.Pattern = "\$.*"," applies the pattern that will be matched by setting the property. The fourteenth code line, "curTaxes = "$178"" is the string that will be searched. The eighteenth code line, "objRegExp.**Replace** (curTaxes, "$0")," finds the data within string, "curTaxes," then replaces the occurrence with zero dollars "$0."

Chapter 5 will cover the following regarding regular expressions:

- ✓ RegExp Object
- ✓ RegExp Properties
- ✓ RegExp Methods
- ✓ Matches Collection Object
- ✓ Match Object
- ✓ Regular Expression Characters

RegExp Object

The RegExp object is a built-in object which provides regular expressions to automation engineers. This object finds regular expression matches in strings, then replace the matches with other strings. One or more instances must be created to use the RegExp object. The following is the syntax for creating a RegExp object:

Syntax
Dim objRegExp
Set objRegExp = **New** RegExp

All of the regular expression properties and methods are accessed through the RegExp object. The following table shows three RegExp object properties and three methods:

3 Tips To Master QTP/UFT Within 30 Days
http://tinyurl.com/3-Tips-For-QTP-UFT

Free Webinars, Videos, and Live Trainings
http://tinyurl.com/Free-QTP-UFT-Selenium

Figure 5.4 – RegExp Properties and Methods

Properties	Methods
Global	Execute
IgnoreCase	Replace
Pattern	Test

RegExp Properties

As discussed in the RegExp Object section, there are three RegExp properties:

- o Global
- o IgnoreCase
- o Pattern

Global

The Global property sets or returns a Boolean value. Boolean values specify if a pattern matches the first occurrence or all occurrences in the search string. The following is the syntax for Global property:

Syntax
Object.**Global** [= Value]

Figure 5.5 – Global Property Syntax Details

Argument	Description
Object	Always a RegExp object
Value	Default is False. True: Search applies to the entire string False: Search applies to the first occurrence

The following example utilizes the Global property via True:

Skype: rex.jones34
Twitter: @RexJonesII
Email: Rex.Jones@Test4Success.org
LinkedIn: https://www.linkedin.com/in/rexjones34

Figure 5.6 - Screenshot of Sample Code

```
1   Option Explicit
2
3   Dim strString
4   Dim objRegExp
5
6   Set objRegExp = New RegExp
7
8   objRegExp.Pattern = "Functional Automation"
9   objRegExp.Global = True
10  strString = "Functional Automation is fast because Functional Automation executes test scripts."
11  MsgBox strString
12  MsgBox objRegExp.Replace (strString, "UFT")
```

Option Explicit

Dim strString
Dim objRegExp

Set objRegExp = **New** RegExp

objRegExp.Pattern = "Functional Automation"
objRegExp.**Global** = **True**
strString = "Functional Automation is fast because Functional Automation executes test scripts."
MsgBox strString
MsgBox objRegExp.**Replace** (strString, "UFT")

- o The first output displays, "Functional Automation is fast because Functional Automation executes test scripts."
- o The second output displays, "UFT is fast because UFT executes test scripts."

3 Tips To Master QTP/UFT Within 30 Days
http://tinyurl.com/3-Tips-For-QTP-UFT

Free Webinars, Videos, and Live Trainings
http://tinyurl.com/Free-QTP-UFT-Selenium

Figure 5.7 - Screenshots Displaying Output from Above Code

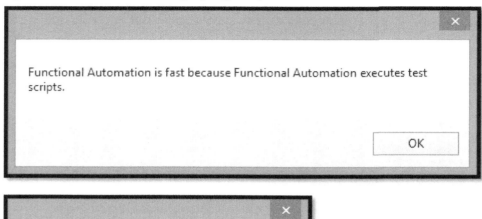

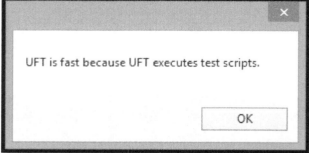

UFT replaces all occurrences of Functional Automation. The following example utilizes the Global property via False:

Chapter 5
Regular Expressions   You Must Learn VBScript for QTP/UFT

Figure 5.8 - Screenshot of Sample Code

```
1    Option Explicit
2
3    Dim strString
4    Dim objRegExp
5
6    Set objRegExp = New RegExp
7
8    objRegExp.Pattern = "Functional Automation"
9    objRegExp.Global = False
10   strString = "Functional Automation is fast because Functional Automation executes test scripts."
11   MsgBox strString
12   MsgBox objRegExp.Replace (strString, "UFT")
```

Option Explicit

Dim strString
Dim objRegExp

Set objRegExp = **New** RegExp

objRegExp.Pattern = "Functional Automation"
objRegExp.**Global** = **False**
strString = "Functional Automation is fast because Functional Automation executes test scripts."
MsgBox strString
MsgBox objRegExp.**Replace** (strString, "UFT")

- o The first output displays, "Functional Automation is fast because Functional Automation executes test scripts."
- o The second output displays, "UFT is fast because Functional Automation executes test scripts."

3 Tips To Master QTP/UFT Within 30 Days
http://tinyurl.com/3-Tips-For-QTP-UFT

Free Webinars, Videos, and Live Trainings
http://tinyurl.com/Free-QTP-UFT-Selenium

Figure 5.9 - Screenshots Displaying Output from Above Code

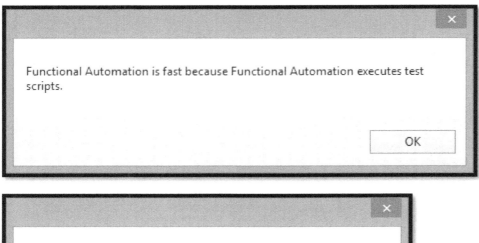

UFT only replaces the first occurrence of Functional Automation while using False as the value for Global.

IgnoreCase
The IgnoreCase property sets or returns a Boolean value. Boolean values specify if a pattern search is case-sensitive. The following is the syntax for IgnoreCase property:

Syntax
Object.IgnoreCase [= Value]

Figure 5.10 – IgnoreCase Property Syntax Details

Argument	Description
Object	Always a RegExp object
Value	Default is False. True: Search is not case sensitive False: Search is case sensitive

The following example utilizes the IgnoreCase property via True:

Figure 5.11 - Screenshot of Sample Code

```
1    Option Explicit
2
3    Dim strString
4    Dim objRegExp
5
6    Set objRegExp = New RegExp
7
8    objRegExp.Pattern = "Functional Automation"
9    objRegExp.Global = True
10   objRegExp.IgnoreCase = True
11   strString = "Functional automation is fast because functional automation executes test scripts."
12   MsgBox strString
13   MsgBox objRegExp.Replace (strString, "UFT")
```

Option Explicit

Dim strString
Dim objRegExp

Set objRegExp = **New** RegExp

objRegExp.Pattern = "Functional Automation"
objRegExp.**Global** = **True**

3 Tips To Master QTP/UFT Within 30 Days
http://tinyurl.com/3-Tips-For-QTP-UFT

Free Webinars, Videos, and Live Trainings
http://tinyurl.com/Free-QTP-UFT-Selenium

objRegExp.IgnoreCase = **True**
strString = "Functional automation is fast because functional automation executes test scripts."
MsgBox strString
MsgBox objRegExp.**Replace** (strString, "UFT")

- o The first output displays, "Functional automation is fast because functional automation executes test scripts."
- o The second output displays, "UFT is fast because UFT executes test scripts."

Figure 5.12 - Screenshots Displaying Output from Above Code

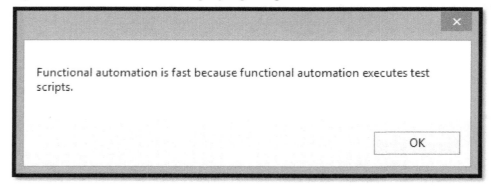

Chapter 5
Regular Expressions   You Must Learn VBScript for QTP/UFT

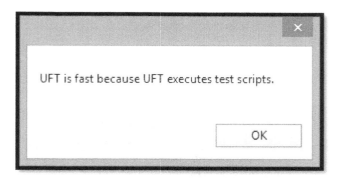

UFT replaces all occurrences of Functional automation. The following example utilizes the IgnoreCase property via False:

Figure 5.13 - Screenshot of Sample Code

```
1    Option Explicit
2
3    Dim strString
4    Dim objRegExp
5
6    Set objRegExp = New RegExp
7
8    objRegExp.Pattern = "Functional Automation"
9    objRegExp.Global = True
10   objRegExp.IgnoreCase = False
11   strString = "Functional automation is fast because functional automation executes test scripts."
12   MsgBox strString
13   MsgBox objRegExp.Replace (strString, "UFT")
```

Option Explicit

Dim strString
Dim objRegExp

Set objRegExp = **New** RegExp

3 Tips To Master QTP/UFT Within 30 Days
http://tinyurl.com/3-Tips-For-QTP-UFT

Free Webinars, Videos, and Live Trainings
http://tinyurl.com/Free-QTP-UFT-Selenium

Chapter 5
Regular Expressions   You Must Learn VBScript for QTP/UFT

objRegExp.Pattern = "Functional Automation"
objRegExp.**Global** = **True**
objRegExp.IgnoreCase = **False**
strString = "Functional automation is fast because functional automation executes test scripts."
MsgBox strString
MsgBox objRegExp.**Replace** (strString, "UFT")

- o The first output displays, "Functional automation is fast because functional automation executes test scripts."
- o The second output displays, "Functional automation is fast because functional automation executes test scripts."

Figure 5.14 - Screenshots Displaying Output from Above Code

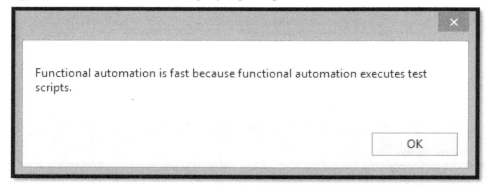

UFT does not replace any occurrences of Functional automation while using False as the value for IgnoreCase.

Pattern

The Pattern property sets or returns the regular expression that will be searched. The following is the syntax for Pattern property:

Skype: rex.jones34
Twitter: @RexJonesII
Email: Rex.Jones@Test4Success.org
LinkedIn: https://www.linkedin.com/in/rexjones34

Syntax
Object.Pattern [= "SearchString"]

Figure 5.15 – Pattern Property Syntax Details

Argument	Description
Object	Always a RegExp object
SearchString	Regular string expression that will be searched (can include regular expression characters).

All of the previous examples used the Pattern property. The following screenshot shows the Pattern property along with Global and IgnoreCase:

Figure 5.16 – Screenshot of Sample Code via Figure 5.11

```
1    Option Explicit
2
3    Dim strString
4    Dim objRegExp
5
6    Set objRegExp = New RegExp
7
8    objRegExp.Pattern = "Functional Automation"
9    objRegExp.Global = True
10   objRegExp.IgnoreCase = True
11   strString = "Functional automation is fast because functional automation executes test scripts."
12   MsgBox strString
13   MsgBox objRegExp.Replace (strString, "UFT")
```

RegExp Methods

As discussed in the RegExp Object section, there are three RegExp methods:

1. Execute
2. Replace
3. Test

3 Tips To Master QTP/UFT Within 30 Days
http://tinyurl.com/3-Tips-For-QTP-UFT

Free Webinars, Videos, and Live Trainings
http://tinyurl.com/Free-QTP-UFT-Selenium

Execute

The Execute method executes a regular expression search against a specified string and always returns a <u>Matches</u> collection. It is possible for the <u>Matches</u> collection to return an empty collection. Each pattern for the regular expression search is set by utilizing the <u>Pattern</u> property. The following is the syntax for the Execute method:

Syntax
Object.**Execute(String)**

Figure 5.17 – Execute Method Syntax Details

Argument	Description
Object	Always a RegExp object
String	A text string or variable that will be searched

The following example utilizes the Execute method:

Skype: rex.jones34
Twitter: @RexJonesII
Email: Rex.Jones@Test4Success.org
LinkedIn: https://www.linkedin.com/in/rexjones34

Figure 5.18 – Screenshot of Sample Code

```
1    Option Explicit
2
3    Dim strString
4    Dim objRegExp, objMatch
5    Dim collMatches
6
7    Set objRegExp = New RegExp
8
9    objRegExp.Global = True
10   objRegExp.Pattern = "[1-4]"
11   strString = "The benefits of automation are:"
12   strString = strString & vbCrLf & vbCrLf & "1.  Fast"
13   strString = strString & vbCrLf & "2.  Effective"
14   strString = strString & vbCrLf & "3.  Accurate"
15   strString = strString & vbCrLf & "4.  Reliable"
16   strString = strString & vbCrLf & "5.  Not True - Automation replaces manual testers"
17
18   MsgBox strString
19
20   Set collMatches = objRegExp.Execute(strString)
21
22   For Each objMatch In collMatches
23       MsgBox "The automation benefit value match is:  " & objMatch.Value
24   Next
```

Option Explicit

Dim strString
Dim objRegExp, objMatch
Dim collMatches

Set objRegExp = **New** RegExp

objRegExp.**Global** = **True**

3 Tips To Master QTP/UFT Within 30 Days
http://tinyurl.com/3-Tips-For-QTP-UFT

Free Webinars, Videos, and Live Trainings
http://tinyurl.com/Free-QTP-UFT-Selenium

```
objRegExp.Pattern = "[1-4]"
strString = "The benefits of automation are:"
strString = strString & vbCrLf & vbCrLf & "1.  Fast"
strString = strString & vbCrLf & "2.  Effective"
strString = strString & vbCrLf & "3.  Accurate"
strString = strString & vbCrLf & "4.  Reliable"
strString = strString & vbCrLf & "5.  Not True - Automation replaces manual testers"


MsgBox strString

Set collMatches = objRegExp.Execute(strString)


For Each objMatch In collMatches
    MsgBox "The automation benefit value match is:  " & objMatch.Value
Next
```

- o The first output is, "The benefits of automation are: 1. Fast / 2. Effective / 3. Accurate / 4. Reliable / 5. Not True – Automation replaces manual testers"
- o The second output displays, "The automation benefit value match is: 1."
- o The third output displays, "The automation benefit value match is: 2."
- o The fourth output displays, "The automation benefit value match is: 3."
- o The fifth output displays, "The automation benefit value match is: 4."

Chapter 5
Regular Expressions   You Must Learn VBScript for QTP/UFT

Figure 5.19 – Screenshots Displaying Output from Above Code

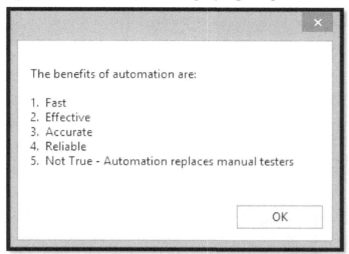

Chapter 5
Regular Expressions   You Must Learn VBScript for QTP/UFT

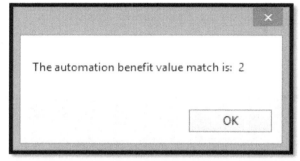

Skype: rex.jones34
Twitter: @RexJonesII
Email: Rex.Jones@Test4Success.org
LinkedIn: https://www.linkedin.com/in/rexjones34

Chapter 5
Regular Expressions   You Must Learn VBScript for QTP/UFT

The Execute method runs a pattern match "[1-4]" for all strings. As a result, the collection "collMatches" returns four matches. Notice, the final string that includes the number 5 does not have an output because there is not a pattern match.

Replace
The Replace method is used to replace data located in a regular expression search. This method was used throughout the RegExp Properties section. The following is the syntax for the Replace method:

Syntax
Object.Replace(String1, String2)

3 Tips To Master QTP/UFT Within 30 Days
http://tinyurl.com/3-Tips-For-QTP-UFT

Free Webinars, Videos, and Live Trainings
http://tinyurl.com/Free-QTP-UFT-Selenium

Figure 5.20 – Replace Method Syntax Details

Argument	Description
Object	Always a RegExp object
String1	A text string or variable in which the text replacement takes place
String2	A text string which is the replacement text string

The following example utilizes the Replace method:

Figure 5.21 – Screenshot of Sample Code

```
1   Option Explicit
2
3   Dim strString
4   Dim objRegExp
5
6   Set objRegExp = New RegExp
7
8   objRegExp.Pattern = "All"
9   strString = "All companies recognize the value of software testing."
10  MsgBox strString
11  MsgBox objRegExp.Replace (strString, "Not all but some")
12
```

Option Explicit

Dim strString
Dim objRegExp

Set objRegExp = **New** RegExp

objRegExp.Pattern = "All"
strString = "All companies recognize the value of software testing."

Skype: rex.jones34
Twitter: @RexJonesII
Email: Rex.Jones@Test4Success.org
LinkedIn: https://www.linkedin.com/in/rexjones34

MsgBox strString
MsgBox objRegExp.**Replace** (strString, "Not all but some")

- o The first output displays, "All companies recognize the value of software testing."
- o The second output displays, "Not all but some companies recognize the value of software testing."

Figure 5.22 – Screenshots Displaying Output from Above Code

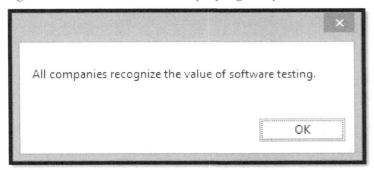

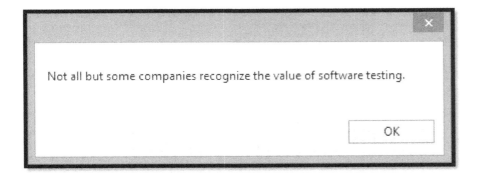

The String2 variable: "Not all but some," replaces the String1 variable: "strString," which includes a value of "All."

Test

The Test method executes a regular expression search against a specified string and returns a Boolean value. Boolean values specify if the pattern match was found. True is returned if a pattern match is found and False is returned if no match is found. The following is the syntax for Test method:

Syntax
Object.Test(**String**)

Figure 5.23 – Test Method Syntax Details

Argument	Description
Object	Always a RegExp object
String	A text string upon which the regular expression is executed.

The following example utilizes the Test method:

Figure 5.24 – Screenshot of Sample Code

```
1    Option Explicit
2
3    Dim strString
4    Dim objRegExp
5
6    Set objRegExp = New RegExp
7
8    objRegExp.Pattern = "QA"
9    strString = "QA Departments are important in the Information Technology (IT) industry."
10
11   If objRegExp.Test(strString) Then
12           MsgBox "True: " & strString
13   Else
14           MsgBox "False: " & strString
15   End If
```

Chapter 5
Regular Expressions   You Must Learn VBScript for QTP/UFT

Option Explicit

Dim strString
Dim objRegExp

Set objRegExp = **New** RegExp

objRegExp.Pattern = "QA"
strString = "QA Departments are important in the Information Technology (IT) industry."

If objRegExp.Test(strString) **Then**
    MsgBox "True: " & strString
Else
    MsgBox "False: " & strString
End If

The output displays, "True: QA Departments are important in the Information Technology (IT) industry."

Figure 5.25 – Screenshot Displaying Output from Above Code

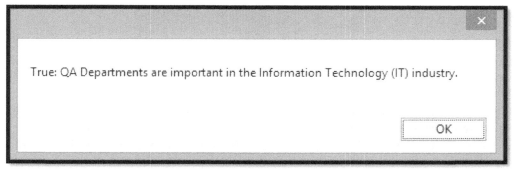

3 Tips To Master QTP/UFT Within 30 Days
http://tinyurl.com/3-Tips-For-QTP-UFT

Free Webinars, Videos, and Live Trainings
http://tinyurl.com/Free-QTP-UFT-Selenium

The Test method returns True so the first message box: "**MsgBox** "True: " & strString,"
displays the output.

Matches Collection Object

The Matches Collection object is a collection of zero or more regular expression Match
objects. Unfortunately, the Execute method of the RegExp object is the only way to create a
Matches Collection object. The Matches Collection object supports two read-only properties:

1. Count
2. Item

Count

The Count property returns the number of Match object items in a collection. The following
example utilizes the Count property:

Figure 5.26 – Screenshot of Sample Code

```
Option Explicit

Dim strString
Dim objRegExp, objMatch
Dim collMatches

Set objRegExp = New RegExp

objRegExp.Global = True
objRegExp.Pattern = "\d"
strString = "The benefits of automation are:"
strString = strString & vbCrLf & vbCrLf & "1.  Fast"
strString = strString & vbCrLf & "2.  Effective"
strString = strString & vbCrLf & "3.  Accurate"
strString = strString & vbCrLf & "4.  Reliable"
strString = strString & vbCrLf & "5.  Not True - Automation replaces manual testers"

MsgBox strString

Set collMatches = objRegExp.Execute(strString)

MsgBox collMatches.Count & " is the item count for this collection."
```

Option Explicit

Dim strString
Dim objRegExp, objMatch
Dim collMatches

Set objRegExp = **New** RegExp

objRegExp.**Global** = **True**
objRegExp.Pattern = "\d"

3 Tips To Master QTP/UFT Within 30 Days
http://tinyurl.com/3-Tips-For-QTP-UFT

Free Webinars, Videos, and Live Trainings
http://tinyurl.com/Free-QTP-UFT-Selenium

strString = "The benefits of automation are:"
strString = strString & **vbCrLf** & **vbCrLf** & "1. Fast"
strString = strString & **vbCrLf** & "2. Effective"
strString = strString & **vbCrLf** & "3. Accurate"
strString = strString & **vbCrLf** & "4. Reliable"
strString = strString & **vbCrLf** & "5. Not True - Automation replaces manual testers"

MsgBox strString

Set collMatches = objRegExp.**Execute**(strString)

MsgBox collMatches.Count & " is the item count for this collection."

- o   The first output displays, "The benefits of automation are: 1. Fast / 2. Effective / 3. Accurate / 4. Reliable / 5. Not True – Automation replaces manual testers"
- o   The second output displays, "5 is the item count for this collection."

Figure 5.27 – Screenshots Displaying Output from Above Code

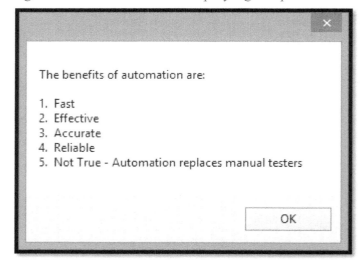

Chapter 5
Regular Expressions   You Must Learn VBScript for QTP/UFT

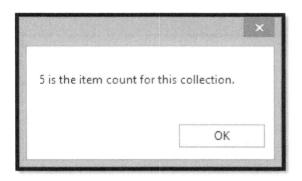

The number of items in this collection is five. The number of items is found by using regular expression character "\d" as the pattern.

Item

The Item property returns the number of Match object items based on a specified key. The following example utilizes the Item property:

Figure 5.28 – Screenshot of Sample Code

```vbscript
1    Option Explicit
2
3    Dim strString
4    Dim objRegExp, objMatch
5    Dim collMatches
6
7    Set objRegExp = New RegExp
8
9    objRegExp.Global = True
10   objRegExp.Pattern = "\d"
11   strString = "The benefits of automation are:"
12   strString = strString & vbCrLf & vbCrLf & "1.  Fast"
13   strString = strString & vbCrLf & "2.  Effective"
14   strString = strString & vbCrLf & "3.  Accurate"
15   strString = strString & vbCrLf & "4.  Reliable"
16   strString = strString & vbCrLf & "5.  Not True - Automation replaces manual testers"
17
18   MsgBox strString
19
20   Set collMatches = objRegExp.Execute(strString)
21
22   MsgBox "What is the first string/number located by the regular expression? " & collMatches.Item(0)
23   MsgBox "What is the second string/number located by the regular expression? " & collMatches.Item(1)
24   MsgBox "What is the third string/number located by the regular expression? " & collMatches.Item(2)
25   MsgBox "What is the fourth string/number located by the regular expression? " & collMatches.Item(3)
26   MsgBox "What is the fifth string/number located by the regular expression? " & collMatches.Item(4)
```

Option Explicit

Dim strString
Dim objRegExp, objMatch
Dim collMatches

Set objRegExp = **New** RegExp

objRegExp.**Global** = **True**
objRegExp.Pattern = "\d"
strString = "The benefits of automation are:"
strString = strString & **vbCrLf** & **vbCrLf** & "1. Fast"

Skype: rex.jones34
Twitter: @RexJonesII
Email: Rex.Jones@Test4Success.org
LinkedIn: https://www.linkedin.com/in/rexjones34

strString = strString & **vbCrLf** & "2. Effective"
strString = strString & **vbCrLf** & "3. Accurate"
strString = strString & **vbCrLf** & "4. Reliable"
strString = strString & **vbCrLf** & "5. Not True - Automation replaces manual testers"

MsgBox strString

Set collMatches = objRegExp.**Execute**(strString)

MsgBox "What is the first string/number located by the regular expression? " & collMatches.Item(0)
MsgBox "What is the second string/number located by the regular expression?
" & collMatches.Item(1)
MsgBox "What is the third string/number located by the regular expression? " & collMatches.Item(2)
MsgBox "What is the fourth string/number located by the regular expression?
" & collMatches.Item(3)
MsgBox "What is the fifth string/number located by the regular expression? " & collMatches.Item(4)

- o The first output displays, "The benefits of automation are: 1. Fast / 2. Effective / 3. Accurate / 4. Reliable / 5. Not True – Automation replaces manual testers."
- o The second output displays, "What is the first string/number located by the regular expression? 1."
- o The third output displays, "What is the second string/number located by the regular expression? 2."
- o The fourth output displays, "What is the third string/number located by the regular expression? 3."
- o The fifth output displays, "What is the fourth string/number located by the regular expression? 4."
- o The sixth output displays, "What is the fifth string/number located by the regular expression? 5."

3 Tips To Master QTP/UFT Within 30 Days
http://tinyurl.com/3-Tips-For-QTP-UFT

Free Webinars, Videos, and Live Trainings
http://tinyurl.com/Free-QTP-UFT-Selenium

Figure 5.29 – Screenshots Displaying Output from Above Code

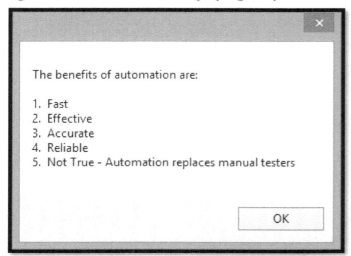

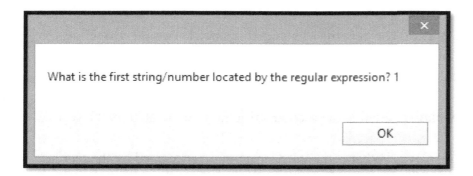

Chapter 5
Regular Expressions

You Must Learn VBScript for QTP/UFT

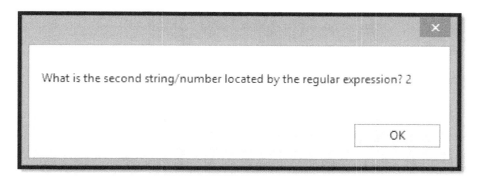

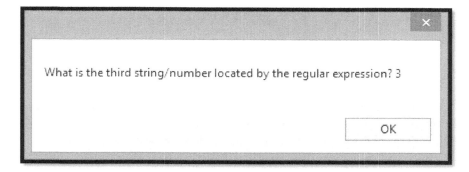

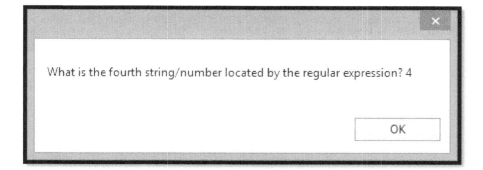

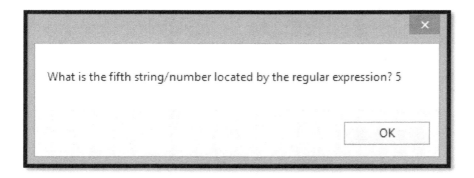

Each string that is a number is located after using the Item property.

Match Object

The Match object is a component in a Matches Collection object. Like the Matches Collection object, a Match object can only be created by using the Execute method of the RegExp object. Each Match object provides access to the following three elements:

1. An index of where the match is located
2. The string that is located by the regular expression
3. The length of the string that is located

The Match object has three read-only properties:

1. FirstIndex
2. Length
3. Value

FirstIndex
The FirstIndex property returns the position within the search string where the match takes place. This property uses a zero-based approach, meaning the first character in every string begins at character zero (0). The following is the syntax for FirstIndex property:

Syntax
Object.FirstIndex

Figure 5.30 – FirstIndex Property Syntax Details

Argument	Description
Object	Always a Match object

Figure 5.31 – Screenshot of Sample Code

```
1    Option Explicit
2
3    Dim strString
4    Dim objRegExp, objMatch
5    Dim collMatches
6
7    Set objRegExp = New RegExp
8
9    objRegExp.Global = True
10   objRegExp.Pattern = "\d"
11   strString = "The benefits of automation are:"
12   strString = strString & vbCrLf & vbCrLf & "1.  Fast"
13   strString = strString & vbCrLf & "2.  Effective"
14   strString = strString & vbCrLf & "3.  Accurate"
15   strString = strString & vbCrLf & "4.  Reliable"
16   strString = strString & vbCrLf & "5.  Not True - Automation replaces manual testers" & vbCrLf & vbCrLf
17
18   Set collMatches = objRegExp.Execute(strString)
19
20   For Each objMatch In collMatches
21          strString = strString & "The first index of Match " & objMatch.Value
22          strString = strString & " is found at position " & objMatch.FirstIndex & "." & vbCrLf
23   Next
24   MsgBox strString
```

Option Explicit

Dim strString
Dim objRegExp, objMatch
Dim collMatches

3 Tips To Master QTP/UFT Within 30 Days
http://tinyurl.com/3-Tips-For-QTP-UFT

Free Webinars, Videos, and Live Trainings
http://tinyurl.com/Free-QTP-UFT-Selenium

```
Set objRegExp = New RegExp

objRegExp.Global = True
objRegExp.Pattern = "\d"
strString = "The benefits of automation are:"
strString = strString & vbCrLf & vbCrLf & "1.  Fast"
strString = strString & vbCrLf & "2.  Effective"
strString = strString & vbCrLf & "3.  Accurate"
strString = strString & vbCrLf & "4.  Reliable"
strString = strString & vbCrLf & "5.  Not True - Automation replaces manual
testers" & vbCrLf & vbCrLf

Set collMatches = objRegExp.Execute(strString)

For Each objMatch In collMatches
    strString = strString & "The first index of Match " & objMatch.Value
    strString = strString & " is found at position " & objMatch.FirstIndex & "." & vbCrLf
Next
MsgBox strString
```

The output displays, "The benefits of automation are: 1. Fast / 2. Effective / 3. Accurate / 4. Reliable / 5. Not True – Automation replaces manual testers / The first index of Match 1 is found at position 34. / The first index of Match 2 is found at position 44. / The first index of Match 3 is found at position 59. / The first index of Match 4 is found at position 73. The first index of Match 5 is found at position 87."

Skype: rex.jones34
Twitter: @RexJonesII
Email: Rex.Jones@Test4Success.org
LinkedIn: https://www.linkedin.com/in/rexjones34

Figure 5.32 – Screenshot Displaying Output from Above Code

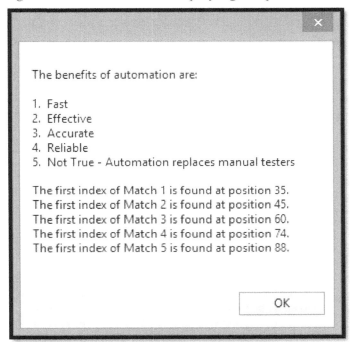

The first index of each match are numbers (1, 2, 3, 4, and 5).

Length

The Length property returns the total length of the matched string. The following is the syntax for Length property:

Syntax
Object.**Length**

Figure 5.33 – Length Property Syntax Details

Argument	Description
Object	Always a Match object

3 Tips To Master QTP/UFT Within 30 Days
http://tinyurl.com/3-Tips-For-QTP-UFT

Free Webinars, Videos, and Live Trainings
http://tinyurl.com/Free-QTP-UFT-Selenium

Figure 5.34 – Screenshot of Sample Code

```
1    Option Explicit
2
3    Dim strString
4    Dim objRegExp, objMatch
5    Dim collMatches
6
7    Set objRegExp = New RegExp
8
9    objRegExp.Global = True
10   objRegExp.Pattern = "\d"
11   strString = "The benefits of automation are:"
12   strString = strString & vbCrLf & vbCrLf & "1.  Fast"
13   strString = strString & vbCrLf & "2.  Effective"
14   strString = strString & vbCrLf & "3.  Accurate"
15   strString = strString & vbCrLf & "4.  Reliable"
16   strString = strString & vbCrLf & "5.  Not True - Automation replaces manual testers" & vbCrLf & vbCrLf
17
18   Set collMatches = objRegExp.Execute(strString)
19
20   For Each objMatch In collMatches
21          strString = strString & "The total length of Match " & "'" & objMatch.Value & "'"
22          strString = strString & " is " & objMatch.Length & "." & vbCrLf
23   Next
24   MsgBox strString
```

Option Explicit

Dim strString
Dim objRegExp, objMatch
Dim collMatches

Set objRegExp = **New** RegExp

objRegExp.**Global** = **True**
objRegExp.Pattern = "\d"
strString = "The benefits of automation are:"
strString = strString & **vbCrLf** & **vbCrLf** & "1. Fast"

Skype: rex.jones34
Twitter: @RexJonesII
Email: Rex.Jones@Test4Success.org
LinkedIn: https://www.linkedin.com/in/rexjones34

strString = strString & **vbCrLf** & "2. Effective"
strString = strString & **vbCrLf** & "3. Accurate"
strString = strString & **vbCrLf** & "4. Reliable"
strString = strString & **vbCrLf** & "5. Not True - Automation replaces manual
testers" & **vbCrLf** & **vbCrLf**

Set collMatches = objRegExp.**Execute**(strString)

For Each objMatch **In** collMatches
    strString = strString & "The total length of Match " & "'" & objMatch.Value & "'"
    strString = strString & " is " & objMatch.**Length** & "." & **vbCrLf**
Next
MsgBox strString

The output displays, "The benefits of automation are: 1. Fast / 2. Effective / 3. Accurate / 4. Reliable / 5. Not True – Automation replaces manual testers / The total length of Match '1' is 1. / The total length of Match '2' is 1. / The total length of Match '3' is 1. / The total length of Match '4' is 1. / The total length of Match '5' is 1."

Figure 5.35 – Screenshot Displaying Output from Above Code

The total length of each match is one for numbers 1, 2, 3, 4, and 5.

Value

The Value property returns the matched value or text in a search string. This property was utilized in the FirstIndex and Length sections. The following are screenshots reiterating the Value property from both sections:

Figure 5.36 – Screenshots of Sample Codes via Figure 5.31 and Figure 5.34

```
1    Option Explicit
2
3    Dim strString
4    Dim objRegExp, objMatch
5    Dim collMatches
6
7    Set objRegExp = New RegExp
8
9    objRegExp.Global = True
10   objRegExp.Pattern = "\d"
11   strString = "The benefits of automation are:"
12   strString = strString & vbCrLf & vbCrLf & "1.  Fast"
13   strString = strString & vbCrLf & "2.  Effective"
14   strString = strString & vbCrLf & "3.  Accurate"
15   strString = strString & vbCrLf & "4.  Reliable"
16   strString = strString & vbCrLf & "5.  Not True - Automation replaces manual testers" & vbCrLf & vbCrLf
17
18   Set collMatches = objRegExp.Execute(strString)
19
20   For Each objMatch In collMatches
21        strString = strString & "The first index of Match " & objMatch.Value
22        strString = strString & " is found at position " & objMatch.FirstIndex & "." & vbCrLf
23   Next
24   MsgBox strString
```

3 Tips To Master QTP/UFT Within 30 Days
http://tinyurl.com/3-Tips-For-QTP-UFT

Free Webinars, Videos, and Live Trainings
http://tinyurl.com/Free-QTP-UFT-Selenium

```
1    Option Explicit
2
3    Dim strString
4    Dim objRegExp, objMatch
5    Dim collMatches
6
7    Set objRegExp = New RegExp
8
9    objRegExp.Global = True
10   objRegExp.Pattern = "\d"
11   strString = "The benefits of automation are:"
12   strString = strString & vbCrLf & vbCrLf & "1.  Fast"
13   strString = strString & vbCrLf & "2.  Effective"
14   strString = strString & vbCrLf & "3.  Accurate"
15   strString = strString & vbCrLf & "4.  Reliable"
16   strString = strString & vbCrLf & "5.  Not True - Automation replaces manual testers" & vbCrLf & vbCrLf
17
18   Set collMatches = objRegExp.Execute(strString)
19
20   For Each objMatch In collMatches
21        strString = strString & "The total length of Match " & "'" & objMatch.Value & "'"
22        strString = strString & " is " & objMatch.Length & "." & vbCrLf
23   Next
24   MsgBox strString
```

Regular Expression Characters

The Regular Expression Characters are special characters used to create a pattern. Special characters that are upper case perform the opposite of their lower case counterparts. The following is a regular expression Character Class example:

Skype: rex.jones34
Twitter: @RexJonesII
Email: Rex.Jones@Test4Success.org
LinkedIn: https://www.linkedin.com/in/rexjones34

Chapter 5
Regular Expressions   You Must Learn VBScript for QTP/UFT

Figure 5.37 – Character Class Example

```
1    Option Explicit
2
3    Dim strString
4    Dim objRegExp
5
6    Set objRegExp = New RegExp
7
8    objRegExp.Pattern = "[1234567]"
9    strString = "It snowed 2 days in New York last week."
10   MsgBox strString
11   MsgBox objRegExp.Replace (strString, "several")
```

Option Explicit

Dim strString
Dim objRegExp

Set objRegExp = **New** RegExp

objRegExp.Pattern = "[1234567]"
strString = "It snowed 2 days in New York last week."
MsgBox strString
MsgBox objRegExp.**Replace** (strString, "several")

- o The first output displays, "It snowed 2 days in New York last week."
- o The second output displays, "It snowed several days in New York last week."

3 Tips To Master QTP/UFT Within 30 Days
http://tinyurl.com/3-Tips-For-QTP-UFT

Free Webinars, Videos, and Live Trainings
http://tinyurl.com/Free-QTP-UFT-Selenium

Figure 5.38 - Screenshots Displaying Output from Above Code

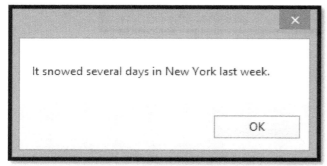

The regular expression characters replaced number 2 with the text "several." For this situation, the pattern could have been shortened by entering [1-7] rather than [1234567]. The shortcut pattern \d represents all digits [0-9] while \D represents all non-digit class [^0-9]. Non-digit classes are classes that do not contain digits/numbers.

The following are categories for Regular Expression Characters:

- ○ Positioning
- ○ Literals
- ○ Character Classes
- ○ Repetition
- ○ Alternation and Grouping

Skype: rex.jones34
Twitter: @RexJonesII
Email: Rex.Jones@Test4Success.org
LinkedIn: https://www.linkedin.com/in/rexjones34

      o   <u>BackReferences</u>

Positioning

Positioning is used to guarantee that the regular expressions are positioned in the appropriate spot. The following table displays the Positioning characters:

Figure 5.39 – Positioning Regular Expression Characters

Character	Description
^	Match only the beginning of a string. "^A" matches first with "A" in "An A+ for Allen."
$	Match only the end of a string. "t$" matches the last "t" in "A cat chases the rat"
\b	Matches a word boundary where the position is between the word/letters and a space. "re\b" matches the "re" in "are" but not the "re" in "area"
\B	Matches a non-word boundary where the position is not between the word/letters and a space. re\b matches the "re" in "area" but not the "re" in "are"

Literals

Literals are virtually any style of characters functioning as alphanumeric characters, ACSII, octal characters, hexadecimal characters, UNICODE, or special escaped characters. A back slash "\" is used before special escaped characters within the context of a regular expression. The following table displays the Literal characters:

Figure 5.40 – Literal Regular Expression Characters

Character	Description
Alphanumeric	Matches alphabetical and numerical characters only.
\n	Matches a new line.

3 Tips To Master QTP/UFT Within 30 Days
http://tinyurl.com/3-Tips-For-QTP-UFT

Free Webinars, Videos, and Live Trainings
http://tinyurl.com/Free-QTP-UFT-Selenium

\f	Matches a form feed.
\r	Matches carriage return
\t	Matches horizontal tab
\v	Matches vertical tab
\?	Matches ?
*	Matches *
\+	Matches +
\.	Matches .
|	Matches |
\{	Matches {
\}	Matches }
\\	Matches \
\[	Matches [
\]	Matches]
\(	Matches (
\)	Matches)
\xxx	Matches the ASCII character expressed by the octal number xxx.
\xdd	Matches the ASCII character expressed by the hex number dd.
\uxxxx	Matches the ASCII character expressed by the UNICODE xxxx.

Character Classes

Character classes permit customized grouping by placing expressions within brackets ([]). A negated character class may be created by placing a caret (^) as the first character inside the brackets. In addition, a dash can be used for a range of characters while some common character sets use a back slash "\" plus a letter. The following table displays the Characters Classes:

Figure 5.41 – Character Classes Regular Expression Characters

Character	**Description**
[xyz]	Matches any one of the enclosed characters in the character set. "[a-e]" matches "b" in "baseball"

Skype: rex.jones34
Twitter: @RexJonesII
Email: Rex.Jones@Test4Success.org
LinkedIn: https://www.linkedin.com/in/rexjones34

[^xyz]	Match any character not enclosed in the character set. "[^a-e]" matches "s" in "baseball"
.	Matches any character except the newline character \n. 1.3 matches "123" "133" and "1-3"
\w	Match any word including the underscore. Equivalent to [a-zA-Z_0-9]
\W	Match any non-word character. Equivalent to [^a-zA-Z_0-9]
\d	Match any digit class. Equivalent to [0-9].
\D	Match any non-digit class. Equivalent to [^0-9]
\s	Match any space character class. Equivalent to [\t\r\n\v\f]
\S	Match any space character class. Equivalent to [^\t\r\n\v\f]

Repetition

Repetition permits multiple searches within a regular expression. In addition, repetition determines the number of times an element can be repeated in a regular expression. The following table displays the Repetition characters:

Figure 5.42 – Repetition Regular Expression Characters

Character	**Description**
*	Matches the preceding character zero or more times. Equivalent to {0,}
+	Matches the preceding character one or more times. Equivalent to {1,}
?	Matches the preceding character zero or one time. "a\s?b" matches "ab" or "a b"
{n}	Match exactly "n" occurrences of a regular expression. "\d{4}" matches 4 digits
{n,}	Match n or more occurrences of a regular expression. "\s{3,}" matches at least 3 space characters
{n,m}	Matches n to m number of occurrences of a regular expression. "\d{4,5}" matches at least 4, but no more than 5 digits

Alternation and Grouping

Alternation and grouping is used to develop complex regular expressions. These characters can create intricate clauses within a regular expression. The following table displays the Alternation and Grouping characters:

Figure 5.43 – Alternation and Grouping Regular Expression Characters

Character	Description
0	Grouping a clause to create a clause. "(xy)?(z)" matches "xyz" or "z"
|	Alternation combines clauses into one regular expression and then matches any of the individual clauses. "(ab)|(cd)|(ef)" matches "ab" or "cd" or "ef"

BackReferences

BackReferences refer back to a portion of the regular expression. The following table displays the BackReferences characters:

Figure 5.44 – BackReference Regular Expression Characters

Character	Description
()\n	Matches a clause as numbered by the left parenthesis. "(\w+)\s+\1" matches any word that occurs twice in a row, such as "hubba hubba"

Chapter 5 explained the benefits of utilizing regular expressions. An automation engineer no longer writes several lines of code to search and replace data but uses regular expressions via RegExp object. The RegExp object has three properties: Global, IgnoreCase, and Pattern and three methods: Execute, Replace, and Test. Chapter 6 will discuss the process of debugging and handling errors.

Skype: rex.jones34
Twitter: @RexJonesII
Email: Rex.Jones@Test4Success.org
LinkedIn: https://www.linkedin.com/in/rexjones34

Chapter 6
Debugging and Handling Errors

It is beneficial for automation engineers to learn the syntax of VBScript. However, even a skilled automation engineer makes syntax errors in their programming. Therefore, automation engineers must acquire an ability to debug and handle errors. Debugging is the process of finding and fixing programming errors. Error-handling is the process of anticipating, detecting, and resolving errors.

Chapter 6 will cover the following information regarding debugging and handling errors:

- ✓ Error Types
- ✓ Debugging
- ✓ Error-Handling

Error Types

All programs deals with errors. Errors are unexpected conditions in the program. The most common errors originate from an automation engineer's code. VBScript has the following three types of errors:

1. Syntax Errors
2. Runtime Errors
3. Logical Errors

Syntax Errors

Syntax errors stop the execution of a program. An unclosed loop is an example of a syntax error. Usually syntax errors are discovered during the development phase when the code is saved. The following is an example that will produce a syntax error:

3 Tips To Master QTP/UFT Within 30 Days
http://tinyurl.com/3-Tips-For-QTP-UFT

Free Webinars, Videos, and Live Trainings
http://tinyurl.com/Free-QTP-UFT-Selenium

Chapter 6
Debugging and Handling Errors   You Must Learn VBScript for QTP/UFT

Figure 6.1 – Screenshot of Sample Code

```
1    Option Explicit
2
3    Dim strUserName, strPassword
4
5    strUserName = "Test"
6    strPassword = "Test123"
7
8    If strUserName = "Test"
9        MsgBox strPassword
10   End If
```

Option Explicit

Dim strUserName, strPassword

strUserName = "Test"
strPassword = "Test123"

If strUserName = "Test"
    MsgBox strPassword
End If

- o The Error pane displays "Line: 8 / Description: 'Expected Then'"
- o The Error pane displays "Line: 10 / Description: Expected end of statement"

Skype: rex.jones34
Twitter: @RexJonesII
Email: Rex.Jones@Test4Success.org
LinkedIn: https://www.linkedin.com/in/rexjones34

Figure 6.2 – Screenshot Displaying Error from Above Code

!	Line	Description	Item
Errors			
Solution	⃠ Errors: 2	⚠ Warnings: 0	ⓘ Messages: 0
⃠	8	Expected 'Then'	Automation 4 Beginners
⃠	10	Expected end of statement	Automation 4 Beginners

For the most part, syntax errors are quick to locate because QTP/UFT provides valuable information regarding the error. In this case, line 8 does not possess the required Then statement within the If-Then statement. The following cause QTP/UFT to highlight a syntax error:

o   Keyword is misspelled
o   Keyword is used incorrectly
o   Keywords, parentheses, statements, etc. are missing from the code

Runtime Errors

Runtime errors are detected when a program executes an invalid action. Therefore, this type of error is not detected upon saving the code because the code is syntactically correct. The following are types of runtime errors:

o   Native Errors
o   Option Explicit Errors

Native Errors

Native errors are errors inherent in VBScript. Errors such as passing a Null value to a function is a native error. The following is an example of a Native Error:

3 Tips To Master QTP/UFT Within 30 Days
http://tinyurl.com/3-Tips-For-QTP-UFT

Free Webinars, Videos, and Live Trainings
http://tinyurl.com/Free-QTP-UFT-Selenium

Chapter 6
Debugging and Handling Errors   You Must Learn VBScript for QTP/UFT

Figure 6.3 – Screenshot of Sample Code

```
1    Option Explicit
2
3    Dim intAvgPrice
4
5    intAvgPrice = 100/0
```

Option Explicit

Dim intAvgPrice

intAvgPrice = 100/0

A Run Error displays, "Division by zero."

Figure 6.4 – Screenshot Displaying Error from Above Code

Most runtime errors provide useful information to assist an automation engineer in locating the problem. In this situation a number (100) cannot be divided by zero. Therefore, a native error occurs because the action is invalid.

Skype: rex.jones34
Twitter: @RexJonesII
Email: Rex.Jones@Test4Success.org
LinkedIn: https://www.linkedin.com/in/rexjones34

Option Explicit Errors

Option Explicit errors are errors related to the keyword Option Explicit. Option Explicit errors appear when some code refers to a variable that has not been declared. The following is an example of an Option Explicit error:

Figure 6.5 – Screenshot of Sample Code

```
1   Option Explicit
2
3   Dim strUserName
4
5   strUserName = "Test"
6
7   If strUserName = "Test" Then
8       MsgBox strPassword
9   End If
```

Option Explicit

Dim strUserName

strUserName = "Test"

If strUserName = "Test" **Then**
  MsgBox strPassword
End If

The Run Error displays, "Variable is undefined: 'strPassword'."

Figure 6.6 – Screenshot Displaying Error from Above Code

Line 8 produces an Option Explicit error because the code attempts to display an output via "MsgBox strPassword." However, the variable "strPassword" was not declared in the Dim statement "line 3."

Logical Errors

Logical errors are errors hidden in the code. A logical error does not generate an error message, instead it fails to function as intended. A logical error can potentially go unnoticed for a long time because there is no error message. The following Mercury Tours Book A Flight page will be used as an example to illustrate a logical error:

Chapter 6
Debugging and Handling Errors   You Must Learn VBScript for QTP/UFT

Figure 6.7 – Mercury Tours Book A Flight Page

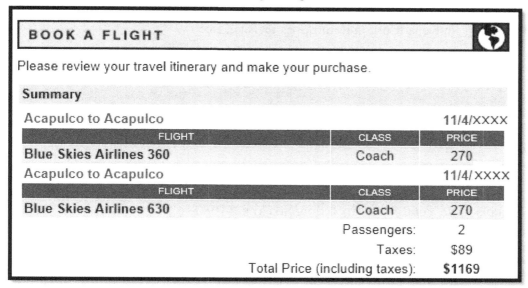

The following is an example of a logical error:

Figure 6.8 – Screenshot of Sample Code

```
1    Option Explicit
2
3    Dim intNumPassengers, intDepartCost, intReturnCost, intTotalPrice
4
5    intNumPassengers = 2
6    intDepartCost = 270
7    intReturnCost = 270
8
9    intTotalPrice = intNumPassengers * (intDepartCost + intReturnCost)
10
11   MsgBox "The Total Price (including taxes) is $" & intTotalPrice
12
```

Option Explicit

Dim intNumPassengers, intDepartCost, intReturnCost, intTotalPrice

intNumPassengers = 2
intDepartCost = 270
intReturnCost = 270

intTotalPrice = intNumPassengers * (intDepartCost + intReturnCost)

MsgBox "The Total Price (including taxes) is $" & intTotalPrice

The output displays "The Total Price (including taxes) is $1080."

Figure 6.9 – Screenshot Displaying Incorrect Result

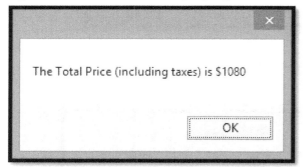

The output displayed a value but it was an incorrect value of $1080. Taxes were not included in the calculation: "intTotalPrice = intNumPassengers * (intDepartCost + intReturnCost)." Logical errors are corrected under while testing and debugging of the code. If not corrected, the code executes successfully every time with an incorrect result. The following examples display the correct code and results:

Skype: rex.jones34
Twitter: @RexJonesII
Email: Rex.Jones@Test4Success.org
LinkedIn: https://www.linkedin.com/in/rexjones34

Chapter 6
Debugging and Handling Errors   You Must Learn VBScript for QTP/UFT

Figure 6.10 – Screenshot of Sample Code

```
 1   Option Explicit
 2
 3   Dim intNumPassengers, intDepartCost, intReturnCost, intTotalPrice, intTaxes, intTotalPlusTaxes
 4
 5   intNumPassengers = 2
 6   intDepartCost = 270
 7   intReturnCost = 270
 8   intTaxes = 89
 9
10   intTotalPrice = intNumPassengers * (intDepartCost + intReturnCost)
11   intTotalPlusTaxes = intTotalPrice + intTaxes
12
13   MsgBox "The Total Price before taxes is $" & intTotalPrice
14   MsgBox "The Total Price (including taxes) is $" & intTotalPlusTaxes
15
```

Option Explicit

Dim intNumPassengers, intDepartCost, intReturnCost, intTotalPrice, intTaxes, intTotalPlusTaxes

intNumPassengers = 2
intDepartCost = 270
intReturnCost = 270
intTaxes = 89

intTotalPrice = intNumPassengers * (intDepartCost + intReturnCost)
intTotalPlusTaxes = intTotalPrice + intTaxes

MsgBox "The Total Price before taxes is $" & intTotalPrice
MsgBox "The Total Price (including taxes) is $" & intTotalPlusTaxes

- o The first output displays, "The Total Price before taxes is $1080."
- o The second output displays, "The Total Price (including taxes) is $1169."

3 Tips To Master QTP/UFT Within 30 Days
http://tinyurl.com/3-Tips-For-QTP-UFT

Free Webinars, Videos, and Live Trainings
http://tinyurl.com/Free-QTP-UFT-Selenium

Chapter 6
Debugging and Handling Errors   You Must Learn VBScript for QTP/UFT

Figure 6.11 – Screenshots Displaying Correct Results

The logical error is fixed after adding intTaxes "89" to the following calculation:
intTotalPlusTaxes = intTotalPrice + intTaxes

Debugging

Debugging is when an automation engineer observes and corrects programming errors. The errors are located by using a debugger. A debugger is a tool which helps an automation engineer follow the code's logic as it executes. The following are some benefits of using a debugger:

o   Assist in understanding a how a program operates
o   Allows an opportunity to step through the code one line at a time
o   Ability to view the value of all variables

The following are features of a debugger tool:

o   Set or Clear Breakpoints
o   Step Through The Code
o   View The Call Stack

Skype: rex.jones34
Twitter: @RexJonesII
Email: Rex.Jones@Test4Success.org
LinkedIn: https://www.linkedin.com/in/rexjones34

Set or Clear Breakpoints

Breakpoints are used to stop the execution of a script. The debugger tool allows a breakpoint to be toggled between setting or clearing a breakpoint on a specific line. The following are examples of a breakpoint:

Figure 6.12 – Screenshots of a Breakpoint via Figure 6.10

```
1    Option Explicit
2
3    Dim intNumPassengers, intDepartCost, intReturnCost, intTotalPrice, intTaxes, intTotalPlusTaxes
4
5    intNumPassengers = 2
6    intDepartCost = 270                         Breakpoint set at Line 10
7    intReturnCost = 270
8    intTaxes = 89
9
10   intTotalPrice = intNumPassengers * (intDepartCost + intReturnCost)
11   intTotalPlusTaxes = intTotalPrice + intTaxes
12
13   MsgBox "The Total Price before taxes is $" & intTotalPrice
14   MsgBox "The Total Price (including taxes) is $" & intTotalPlusTaxes
15
16
```

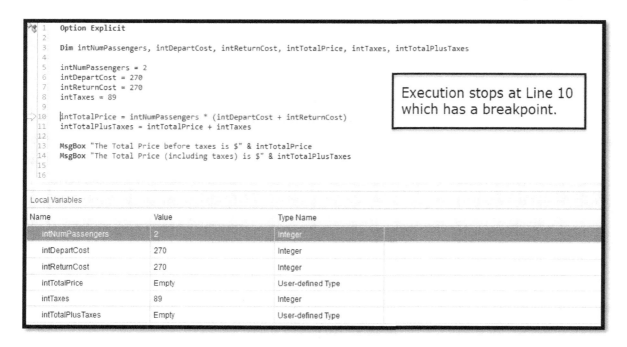

```
 1    Option Explicit
 2
 3    Dim intNumPassengers, intDepartCost, intReturnCost, intTotalPrice, intTaxes, intTotalPlusTaxes
 4
 5    intNumPassengers = 2
 6    intDepartCost = 270
 7    intReturnCost = 270
 8    intTaxes = 89
 9
10    intTotalPrice = intNumPassengers * (intDepartCost + intReturnCost)
11    intTotalPlusTaxes = intTotalPrice + intTaxes
12
13    MsgBox "The Total Price before taxes is $" & intTotalPrice
14    MsgBox "The Total Price (including taxes) is $" & intTotalPlusTaxes
15
16
```

> Execution stops at Line 10 which has a breakpoint.

Local Variables

Name	Value	Type Name
intNumPassengers	2	Integer
intDepartCost	270	Integer
intReturnCost	270	Integer
intTotalPrice	Empty	User-defined Type
intTaxes	89	Integer
intTotalPlusTaxes	Empty	User-defined Type

```
 1    Option Explicit
 2
 3    Dim intNumPassengers, intDepartCost, intReturnCost, intTotalPrice, intTaxes, intTotalPlusTaxes
 4
 5    intNumPassengers = 2
 6    intDepartCost = 270
 7    intReturnCost = 270
 8    intTaxes = 89
 9
10    intTotalPrice = intNumPassengers * (intDepartCost + intReturnCost)
11    intTotalPlusTaxes = intTotalPrice + intTaxes
12
13    MsgBox "The Total Price before taxes is $" & intTotalPrice
14    MsgBox "The Total Price (including taxes) is $" & intTotalPlusTaxes
15
16
```

> Breakpoint has been cleared from Line 10

Chapter 6
Debugging and Handling Errors   You Must Learn VBScript for QTP/UFT

Step through The Code

Stepping through the code is when the debugger steps/executes a line of code one line at a time. Executing a line of code one at a time helps the automation engineer understand how the logic works. The following are three commands for stepping through the code:

1. Step Into
2. Step Out
3. Step Over

The following code will be used to explain all three commands and the Call Stack:

Figure 6.13 – Screenshot of Sample Code

```
1    Option Explicit
2
3    MsgBox "There will be 2 calculations (before taxes and after taxes)"
4    Call CalculateTotalPrice
5    MsgBox "Execution ends after this line"
6
7  ⊟ Sub CalculateTotalPrice
8        Dim intNumPassengers, intDepartCost, intReturnCost, intTotalPrice
9
10       intNumPassengers = 2
11       intDepartCost = 270
12       intReturnCost = 270
13
14       intTotalPrice = intNumPassengers * (intDepartCost + intReturnCost)
15       MsgBox "The Total Price before taxes is $" & intTotalPrice
16
17       CalculateTotalPlusTaxes (intTotalPrice)
18
19   └ End Sub
20
21 ⊟ Function CalculateTotalPlusTaxes (intPriceTotal)
22
23       Dim intTaxes
24       intTaxes = 89
25
26       CalculateTotalPlusTaxes = intPriceTotal + intTaxes
27
28       DisplayTotalPrice (CalculateTotalPlusTaxes)
29
30   └ End Function
31
32 ⊟ Sub DisplayTotalPrice (intTotal)
33       MsgBox "The Total Price (including taxes) is $" & intTotal
34   └ End Sub
```

Option Explicit

MsgBox "There will be 2 calculations (before taxes and after taxes)"

Skype: rex.jones34
Twitter: @RexJonesII
Email: Rex.Jones@Test4Success.org
LinkedIn: https://www.linkedin.com/in/rexjones34

Chapter 6
Debugging and Handling Errors   You Must Learn VBScript for QTP/UFT

```
Call CalculateTotalPrice
MsgBox "Execution ends after this line"

Sub CalculateTotalPrice
    Dim intNumPassengers, intDepartCost, intReturnCost, intTotalPrice

    intNumPassengers = 2
    intDepartCost = 270
    intReturnCost = 270

    intTotalPrice = intNumPassengers * (intDepartCost + intReturnCost)
    MsgBox "The Total Price before taxes is $" & intTotalPrice

    CalculateTotalPlusTaxes (intTotalPrice)

End Sub

Function CalculateTotalPlusTaxes (intPriceTotal)

    Dim intTaxes
    intTaxes = 89

    CalculateTotalPlusTaxes = intPriceTotal + intTaxes

    DisplayTotalPrice (CalculateTotalPlusTaxes)

End Function

Sub DisplayTotalPrice (intTotal)
    MsgBox "The Total Price (including taxes) is $" & intTotal
End Sub
```

3 Tips To Master QTP/UFT Within 30 Days
http://tinyurl.com/3-Tips-For-QTP-UFT

Free Webinars, Videos, and Live Trainings
http://tinyurl.com/Free-QTP-UFT-Selenium

Step Into

The Step Into command executes only the current code line. The debugger pauses at every line of code that is stepped into including a called procedure/function. When a procedure is called from a line of code then the step stops at the procedure's first code line and can continue stepping throughout the procedure via Step Into command. The following screenshots illustrate the Step Into command:

Skype: rex.jones34
Twitter: @RexJonesII
Email: Rex.Jones@Test4Success.org
LinkedIn: https://www.linkedin.com/in/rexjones34

Figure 6.14 – Screenshots for Step Into Command

```
 1    Option Explicit
 2
 3    MsgBox "There will be 2 calculations (before taxes and after taxes)"
 4    Call CalculateTotalPrice
 5    MsgBox "Execution ends after this line"
 6
 7  ⊟ Sub CalculateTotalPrice
 8        Dim intNumPassengers, intDepartCost, intReturnCost, intTotalPrice
 9
10        intNumPassengers = 2
11        intDepartCost = 270
12        intReturnCost = 270
13
14        intTotalPrice = intNumPassengers * (intDepartCost + intReturnCost)
15        MsgBox "The Total Price before taxes is $" & intTotalPrice
16
17        CalculateTotalPlusTaxes (intTotalPrice)
18
19    └ End Sub
20
21  ⊟ Function CalculateTotalPlusTaxes (intPriceTotal)
22
23        Dim intTaxes
24        intTaxes = 89
25
26        CalculateTotalPlusTaxes = intPriceTotal + intTaxes
27
28        DisplayTotalPrice (CalculateTotalPlusTaxes)
29
30    └ End Function
31
32  ⊟ Sub DisplayTotalPrice (intTotal)
33        MsgBox "The Total Price (including taxes) is $" & intTotal
34    └ End Sub
35
```

3 Tips To Master QTP/UFT Within 30 Days
http://tinyurl.com/3-Tips-For-QTP-UFT

Free Webinars, Videos, and Live Trainings
http://tinyurl.com/Free-QTP-UFT-Selenium

Chapter 6
Debugging and Handling Errors   You Must Learn VBScript for QTP/UFT

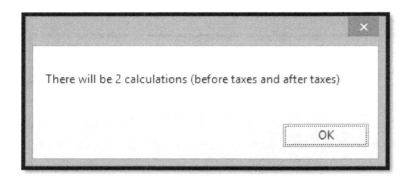

```
1    Option Explicit
2
3    MsgBox "There will be 2 calculations (before taxes and after taxes)"
4    Call CalculateTotalPrice
5    MsgBox "Execution ends after this line"
6
7   ☐ Sub CalculateTotalPrice
8         Dim intNumPassengers, intDepartCost, intReturnCost, intTotalPrice
9
10        intNumPassengers = 2
11        intDepartCost = 270
12        intReturnCost = 270
13
14        intTotalPrice = intNumPassengers * (intDepartCost + intReturnCost)
15        MsgBox "The Total Price before taxes is $" & intTotalPrice
16
17        CalculateTotalPlusTaxes (intTotalPrice)
18
19    └ End Sub
20
21   ☐ Function CalculateTotalPlusTaxes (intPriceTotal)
22
23        Dim intTaxes
24        intTaxes = 89
25
26        CalculateTotalPlusTaxes = intPriceTotal + intTaxes
27
28        DisplayTotalPrice (CalculateTotalPlusTaxes)
29
30    └ End Function
31
32   ☐ Sub DisplayTotalPrice (intTotal)
33        MsgBox "The Total Price (including taxes) is $" & intTotal
34    └ End Sub
35
36
```

3 Tips To Master QTP/UFT Within 30 Days
http://tinyurl.com/3-Tips-For-QTP-UFT

Free Webinars, Videos, and Live Trainings
http://tinyurl.com/Free-QTP-UFT-Selenium

```vbscript
1   Option Explicit
2
3   MsgBox "There will be 2 calculations (before taxes and after taxes)"
4   Call CalculateTotalPrice
5   MsgBox "Execution ends after this line"
6
7   Sub CalculateTotalPrice
8       Dim intNumPassengers, intDepartCost, intReturnCost, intTotalPrice
9
10      intNumPassengers = 2
11      intDepartCost = 270
12      intReturnCost = 270
13
14      intTotalPrice = intNumPassengers * (intDepartCost + intReturnCost)
15      MsgBox "The Total Price before taxes is $" & intTotalPrice
16
17      CalculateTotalPlusTaxes (intTotalPrice)
18
19  End Sub
20
21  Function CalculateTotalPlusTaxes (intPriceTotal)
22
23      Dim intTaxes
24      intTaxes = 89
25
26      CalculateTotalPlusTaxes = intPriceTotal + intTaxes
27
28      DisplayTotalPrice (CalculateTotalPlusTaxes)
29
30  End Function
31
32  Sub DisplayTotalPrice (intTotal)
33      MsgBox "The Total Price (including taxes) is $" & intTotal
34  End Sub
35
```

Skype: rex.jones34
Twitter: @RexJonesII
Email: Rex.Jones@Test4Success.org
LinkedIn: https://www.linkedin.com/in/rexjones34

```
 1    Option Explicit
 2
 3    MsgBox "There will be 2 calculations (before taxes and after taxes)"
 4    Call CalculateTotalPrice
 5    MsgBox "Execution ends after this line"
 6
 7  ⊟ Sub CalculateTotalPrice
 8        Dim intNumPassengers, intDepartCost, intReturnCost, intTotalPrice
 9
10        intNumPassengers = 2
11        intDepartCost = 270
12        intReturnCost = 270
13
14        intTotalPrice = intNumPassengers * (intDepartCost + intReturnCost)
15        MsgBox "The Total Price before taxes is $" & intTotalPrice
16
17        CalculateTotalPlusTaxes (intTotalPrice)
18
19    └ End Sub
20
21  ⊟ Function CalculateTotalPlusTaxes (intPriceTotal)
22
23        Dim intTaxes
24        intTaxes = 89
25
26        CalculateTotalPlusTaxes = intPriceTotal + intTaxes
27
28        DisplayTotalPrice (CalculateTotalPlusTaxes)
29
30    └ End Function
31
32  ⊟ Sub DisplayTotalPrice (intTotal)
33        MsgBox "The Total Price (including taxes) is $" & intTotal
34    └ End Sub
```

Chapter 6
Debugging and Handling Errors   You Must Learn VBScript for QTP/UFT

Explanation of the Step Into Command via Screenshots

- o The first screenshot displays, an execution that begins by using the Step Into which pauses at line 3.

- o The second screenshot displays, "There will be 2 calculations (before taxes and after taxes)." This screenshot appears after stepping through line 3 which is a message box via Step Into command.

- o The third screenshot pauses at line 4.

- o The fourth screenshot pauses at line 10 due to a procedure call "Call CalculateTotalPrice" after stepping through line 4.

- o The fifth screenshot pauses at line 11 after stepping through line 10.

The Step Into command will continue stepping through the code line by line.

Step Out
The Step Out command executes the remaining code lines within a procedure without stepping line by line. After stepping out of the procedure, execution pauses at the code line following the code line that called the procedure. This command can only be used after executing the Step Into command to enter a procedure. The following screenshots illustrate the Step Out command:

Skype: rex.jones34
Twitter: @RexJonesII
Email: Rex.Jones@Test4Success.org
LinkedIn: https://www.linkedin.com/in/rexjones34

Figure 6.15 – Screenshots for Step Out Command

```vbscript
1    Option Explicit
2
3    MsgBox "There will be 2 calculations (before taxes and after taxes)"
4    Call CalculateTotalPrice
5    MsgBox "Execution ends after this line"
6
7  ⊟ Sub CalculateTotalPrice
8        Dim intNumPassengers, intDepartCost, intReturnCost, intTotalPrice
9
10       intNumPassengers = 2
11       intDepartCost = 270
12       intReturnCost = 270
13
14       intTotalPrice = intNumPassengers * (intDepartCost + intReturnCost)
15       MsgBox "The Total Price before taxes is $" & intTotalPrice
16
17       CalculateTotalPlusTaxes (intTotalPrice)
18
19   End Sub
20
21 ⊟ Function CalculateTotalPlusTaxes (intPriceTotal)
22
23       Dim intTaxes
24       intTaxes = 89
25
26       CalculateTotalPlusTaxes = intPriceTotal + intTaxes
27
28       DisplayTotalPrice (CalculateTotalPlusTaxes)
29
30   End Function
31
32 ⊟ Sub DisplayTotalPrice (intTotal)
33       MsgBox "The Total Price (including taxes) is $" & intTotal
34   End Sub
35
```

3 Tips To Master QTP/UFT Within 30 Days
http://tinyurl.com/3-Tips-For-QTP-UFT

Free Webinars, Videos, and Live Trainings
http://tinyurl.com/Free-QTP-UFT-Selenium

Chapter 6
Debugging and Handling Errors
You Must Learn VBScript for QTP/UFT

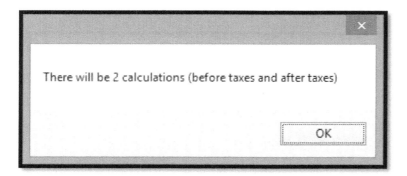

Chapter 6
Debugging and Handling Errors

```vbscript
1    Option Explicit
2
3    MsgBox "There will be 2 calculations (before taxes and after taxes)"
4    Call CalculateTotalPrice
5    MsgBox "Execution ends after this line"
6
7   ⊟ Sub CalculateTotalPrice
8        Dim intNumPassengers, intDepartCost, intReturnCost, intTotalPrice
9
10       intNumPassengers = 2
11       intDepartCost = 270
12       intReturnCost = 270
13
14       intTotalPrice = intNumPassengers * (intDepartCost + intReturnCost)
15       MsgBox "The Total Price before taxes is $" & intTotalPrice
16
17       CalculateTotalPlusTaxes (intTotalPrice)
18
19    └ End Sub
20
21   ⊟ Function CalculateTotalPlusTaxes (intPriceTotal)
22
23       Dim intTaxes
24       intTaxes = 89
25
26       CalculateTotalPlusTaxes = intPriceTotal + intTaxes
27
28       DisplayTotalPrice (CalculateTotalPlusTaxes)
29
30    └ End Function
31
32   ⊟ Sub DisplayTotalPrice (intTotal)
33       MsgBox "The Total Price (including taxes) is $" & intTotal
34    └ End Sub
35
36
```

```
1    Option Explicit
2
3    MsgBox "There will be 2 calculations (before taxes and after taxes)"
4    Call CalculateTotalPrice
5    MsgBox "Execution ends after this line"
6
7  ☐ Sub CalculateTotalPrice
8        Dim intNumPassengers, intDepartCost, intReturnCost, intTotalPrice
9
10       intNumPassengers = 2
11       intDepartCost = 270
12       intReturnCost = 270
13
14       intTotalPrice = intNumPassengers * (intDepartCost + intReturnCost)
15       MsgBox "The Total Price before taxes is $" & intTotalPrice
16
17       CalculateTotalPlusTaxes (intTotalPrice)
18
19   └ End Sub
20
21 ☐ Function CalculateTotalPlusTaxes (intPriceTotal)
22
23       Dim intTaxes
24       intTaxes = 89
25
26       CalculateTotalPlusTaxes = intPriceTotal + intTaxes
27
28       DisplayTotalPrice (CalculateTotalPlusTaxes)
29
30   └ End Function
31
32 ☐ Sub DisplayTotalPrice (intTotal)
33       MsgBox "The Total Price (including taxes) is $" & intTotal
34   └ End Sub
35
```

Skype: rex.jones34
Twitter: @RexJonesII
Email: Rex.Jones@Test4Success.org
LinkedIn: https://www.linkedin.com/in/rexjones34

Chapter 6
Debugging and Handling Errors

You Must Learn VBScript for QTP/UFT

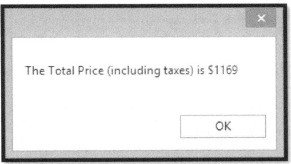

```
  1    Option Explicit
  2
  3    MsgBox "There will be 2 calculations (before taxes and after taxes)"
  4    Call CalculateTotalPrice
  5    MsgBox "Execution ends after this line"
  6
  7  □ Sub CalculateTotalPrice
  8        Dim intNumPassengers, intDepartCost, intReturnCost, intTotalPrice
  9
 10        intNumPassengers = 2
 11        intDepartCost = 270
 12        intReturnCost = 270
 13
 14        intTotalPrice = intNumPassengers * (intDepartCost + intReturnCost)
 15        MsgBox "The Total Price before taxes is $" & intTotalPrice
 16
 17        CalculateTotalPlusTaxes (intTotalPrice)
 18
 19   └ End Sub
 20
 21  □ Function CalculateTotalPlusTaxes (intPriceTotal)
 22
 23        Dim intTaxes
 24        intTaxes = 89
 25
 26        CalculateTotalPlusTaxes = intPriceTotal + intTaxes
 27
 28        DisplayTotalPrice (CalculateTotalPlusTaxes)
 29
 30   └ End Function
 31
 32  □ Sub DisplayTotalPrice (intTotal)
 33        MsgBox "The Total Price (including taxes) is $" & intTotal
 34   └ End Sub
```

Skype: rex.jones34
Twitter: @RexJonesII
Email: Rex.Jones@Test4Success.org
LinkedIn: https://www.linkedin.com/in/rexjones34

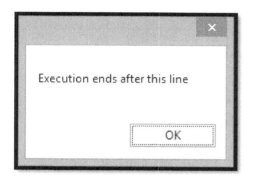

Explanation of the Step Out Command via Screenshots

o   The first screenshot displays, an execution that begins by using the Step Into which pauses at Line 3.
    Note: The Step Out command is not available.

o   The second screenshot displays, "There will be 2 calculations (before taxes and after taxes)." This screenshot appears after stepping through line 3 which is a message box via Step Into command.

o   The third screenshot pauses at line 4.

o   The fourth screenshot pauses at line 10 due to a procedure call "Call CalculateTotalPrice" after stepping through line 4.
    Note: The Step Out command is available since execution is within a procedure "CalculateTotalPrice".

o   The fifth screenshot displays, "The Total Price before taxes is $1080." This screenshot appears after stepping out of the procedure "CalculateTotalPrice". The Step Out command executes code line 15 without stepping through the procedure one code line at a time.

- o The sixth screenshot displays, "The Total Price (including taxes) is $1169." This screenshot appears after stepping out of all procedures "CalculateTotalPrice, CalculateTotalPlusTaxes, and DisplayTotalPrice" but still execute code line "33" within procedure "DisplayTotalPrice."

- o The seventh screenshot pauses at line 5 because line 5 is the code line following a procedure call "Call CalculateTotalPrice" at line 4.

- o The eighth screenshot displays, "Execution ends after this line" after stepping through line 5.

The Step Out command is helpful for automation engineers who do not want to step through the procedure or well-acquainted with a specific procedure.

Step Over
The Step Over command executes only the currently selected line of code line, like the Step Into command. However, there are two scenarios for this command:

1. Sidesteps/avoids a procedure when calling the procedure.
2. Each code line is executed while inside the procedure.

Skype: rex.jones34
Twitter: @RexJonesII
Email: Rex.Jones@Test4Success.org
LinkedIn: https://www.linkedin.com/in/rexjones34

Chapter 6
Debugging and Handling Errors   You Must Learn VBScript for QTP/UFT

Figure 6.16 – Screenshots for Step Over Command (First Scenario)

```vbscript
1   Option Explicit
2
3   MsgBox "There will be 2 calculations (before taxes and after taxes)"
4   Call CalculateTotalPrice
5   MsgBox "Execution ends after this line"
6
7   Sub CalculateTotalPrice
8       Dim intNumPassengers, intDepartCost, intReturnCost, intTotalPrice
9
10      intNumPassengers = 2
11      intDepartCost = 270
12      intReturnCost = 270
13
14      intTotalPrice = intNumPassengers * (intDepartCost + intReturnCost)
15      MsgBox "The Total Price before taxes is $" & intTotalPrice
16
17      CalculateTotalPlusTaxes (intTotalPrice)
18
19  End Sub
20
21  Function CalculateTotalPlusTaxes (intPriceTotal)
22
23      Dim intTaxes
24      intTaxes = 89
25
26      CalculateTotalPlusTaxes = intPriceTotal + intTaxes
27
28      DisplayTotalPrice (CalculateTotalPlusTaxes)
29
30  End Function
31
32  Sub DisplayTotalPrice (intTotal)
33      MsgBox "The Total Price (including taxes) is $" & intTotal
34  End Sub
35
```

3 Tips To Master QTP/UFT Within 30 Days
http://tinyurl.com/3-Tips-For-QTP-UFT

Free Webinars, Videos, and Live Trainings
http://tinyurl.com/Free-QTP-UFT-Selenium

Chapter 6
Debugging and Handling Errors   You Must Learn VBScript for QTP/UFT

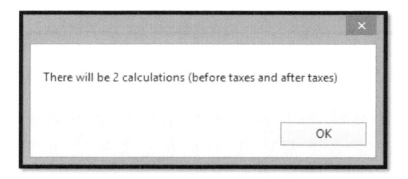

```
1   Option Explicit
2
3   MsgBox "There will be 2 calculations (before taxes and after taxes)"
4   Call CalculateTotalPrice
5   MsgBox "Execution ends after this line"
6
7   Sub CalculateTotalPrice
8       Dim intNumPassengers, intDepartCost, intReturnCost, intTotalPrice
9
10      intNumPassengers = 2
11      intDepartCost = 270
12      intReturnCost = 270
13
14      intTotalPrice = intNumPassengers * (intDepartCost + intReturnCost)
15      MsgBox "The Total Price before taxes is $" & intTotalPrice
16
17      CalculateTotalPlusTaxes (intTotalPrice)
18
19  End Sub
20
21  Function CalculateTotalPlusTaxes (intPriceTotal)
22
23      Dim intTaxes
24      intTaxes = 89
25
26      CalculateTotalPlusTaxes = intPriceTotal + intTaxes
27
28      DisplayTotalPrice (CalculateTotalPlusTaxes)
29
30  End Function
31
32  Sub DisplayTotalPrice (intTotal)
33      MsgBox "The Total Price (including taxes) is $" & intTotal
34  End Sub
```

Chapter 6
Debugging and Handling Errors

You Must Learn VBScript for QTP/UFT

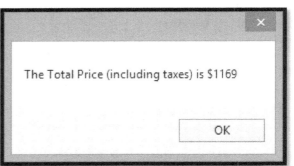

```
1    Option Explicit
2
3    MsgBox "There will be 2 calculations (before taxes and after taxes)"
4    Call CalculateTotalPrice
5    MsgBox "Execution ends after this line"
6
7  ⊟ Sub CalculateTotalPrice
8        Dim intNumPassengers, intDepartCost, intReturnCost, intTotalPrice
9
10       intNumPassengers = 2
11       intDepartCost = 270
12       intReturnCost = 270
13
14       intTotalPrice = intNumPassengers * (intDepartCost + intReturnCost)
15       MsgBox "The Total Price before taxes is $" & intTotalPrice
16
17       CalculateTotalPlusTaxes (intTotalPrice)
18
19   └End Sub
20
21 ⊟ Function CalculateTotalPlusTaxes (intPriceTotal)
22
23       Dim intTaxes
24       intTaxes = 89
25
26       CalculateTotalPlusTaxes = intPriceTotal + intTaxes
27
28       DisplayTotalPrice (CalculateTotalPlusTaxes)
29
30   └End Function
31
32 ⊟ Sub DisplayTotalPrice (intTotal)
33       MsgBox "The Total Price (including taxes) is $" & intTotal
34   └End Sub
35
```

3 Tips To Master QTP/UFT Within 30 Days
http://tinyurl.com/3-Tips-For-QTP-UFT

Free Webinars, Videos, and Live Trainings
http://tinyurl.com/Free-QTP-UFT-Selenium

Chapter 6
Debugging and Handling Errors
You Must Learn VBScript for QTP/UFT

Explanation of the Step Over Command via Screenshots (First Scenario)

o The first screenshot displays, an execution that begins by using the Step Into which
   pauses at Line 3.
   Note: The Step Over command becomes available after pausing at line 3.

o The second screenshot displays, "There will be 2 calculations (before taxes and after
   taxes)." This screenshot appears after stepping through line 3 which is a message box
   via Step Over command.

o The third screenshot pauses at line 4.

o The fourth screenshot displays, "The Total Price before taxes is $1080." This
   screenshot appears after stepping over the procedure "CalculateTotalPrice". The Step
   Over command executes code line 15 without stepping through the procedure one
   code line at a time.

o The fifth screenshot displays, "The Total Price (including taxes) is $1169." This
   screenshot appears after stepping over of all procedures "CalculateTotalPrice,
   CalculateTotalPlusTaxes, and DisplayTotalPrice" but still execute code line "33"
   within procedure "DisplayTotalPrice."

Skype: rex.jones34
Twitter: @RexJonesII
Email: Rex.Jones@Test4Success.org
LinkedIn: https://www.linkedin.com/in/rexjones34

Chapter 6
Debugging and Handling Errors   You Must Learn VBScript for QTP/UFT

- o   The sixth screenshot pauses at line 5 because line 5 is the code line following a procedure call "Call CalculateTotalPrice" at line 4.

- o   The seventh screenshot displays, "Execution ends after this line" after stepping through line 5.

The Step Over command operates like the Step Out command by avoiding all of the procedures but still execute the command lines within the procedures.

Figure 6.17 – Screenshots for Step Over Command (Second Scenario)

```vbscript
1    Option Explicit
2
3    MsgBox "There will be 2 calculations (before taxes and after taxes)"
4    Call CalculateTotalPrice
5    MsgBox "Execution ends after this line"
6
7    Sub CalculateTotalPrice
8        Dim intNumPassengers, intDepartCost, intReturnCost, intTotalPrice
9
10       intNumPassengers = 2
11       intDepartCost = 270
12       intReturnCost = 270
13
14       intTotalPrice = intNumPassengers * (intDepartCost + intReturnCost)
15       MsgBox "The Total Price before taxes is $" & intTotalPrice
16
17       CalculateTotalPlusTaxes (intTotalPrice)
18
19   End Sub
20
21   Function CalculateTotalPlusTaxes (intPriceTotal)
22
23       Dim intTaxes
24       intTaxes = 89
25
26       CalculateTotalPlusTaxes = intPriceTotal + intTaxes
27
28       DisplayTotalPrice (CalculateTotalPlusTaxes)
29
30   End Function
31
32   Sub DisplayTotalPrice (intTotal)
33       MsgBox "The Total Price (including taxes) is $" & intTotal
34   End Sub
```

Chapter 6
Debugging and Handling Errors

You Must Learn VBScript for QTP/UFT

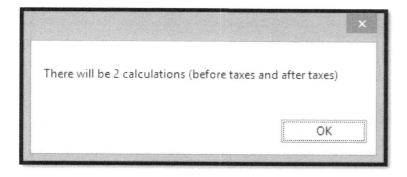

```vbscript
1    Option Explicit
2
3    MsgBox "There will be 2 calculations (before taxes and after taxes)"
4    Call CalculateTotalPrice
5    MsgBox "Execution ends after this line"
6
7    Sub CalculateTotalPrice
8        Dim intNumPassengers, intDepartCost, intReturnCost, intTotalPrice
9
10       intNumPassengers = 2
11       intDepartCost = 270
12       intReturnCost = 270
13
14       intTotalPrice = intNumPassengers * (intDepartCost + intReturnCost)
15       MsgBox "The Total Price before taxes is $" & intTotalPrice
16
17       CalculateTotalPlusTaxes (intTotalPrice)
18
19   End Sub
20
21   Function CalculateTotalPlusTaxes (intPriceTotal)
22
23       Dim intTaxes
24       intTaxes = 89
25
26       CalculateTotalPlusTaxes = intPriceTotal + intTaxes
27
28       DisplayTotalPrice (CalculateTotalPlusTaxes)
29
30   End Function
31
32   Sub DisplayTotalPrice (intTotal)
33       MsgBox "The Total Price (including taxes) is $" & intTotal
34   End Sub
35
36
```

Skype: rex.jones34
Twitter: @RexJonesII
Email: Rex.Jones@Test4Success.org
LinkedIn: https://www.linkedin.com/in/rexjones34

Chapter 6
Debugging and Handling Errors

You Must Learn VBScript for QTP/UFT

```vbscript
 1   Option Explicit
 2
 3   MsgBox "There will be 2 calculations (before taxes and after taxes)"
 4   Call CalculateTotalPrice
 5   MsgBox "Execution ends after this line"
 6
 7   Sub CalculateTotalPrice
 8       Dim intNumPassengers, intDepartCost, intReturnCost, intTotalPrice
 9
10       intNumPassengers = 2
11       intDepartCost = 270
12       intReturnCost = 270
13
14       intTotalPrice = intNumPassengers * (intDepartCost + intReturnCost)
15       MsgBox "The Total Price before taxes is $" & intTotalPrice
16
17       CalculateTotalPlusTaxes (intTotalPrice)
18
19   End Sub
20
21   Function CalculateTotalPlusTaxes (intPriceTotal)
22
23       Dim intTaxes
24       intTaxes = 89
25
26       CalculateTotalPlusTaxes = intPriceTotal + intTaxes
27
28       DisplayTotalPrice (CalculateTotalPlusTaxes)
29
30   End Function
31
32   Sub DisplayTotalPrice (intTotal)
33       MsgBox "The Total Price (including taxes) is $" & intTotal
34   End Sub
35
```

3 Tips To Master QTP/UFT Within 30 Days
http://tinyurl.com/3-Tips-For-QTP-UFT

Free Webinars, Videos, and Live Trainings
http://tinyurl.com/Free-QTP-UFT-Selenium

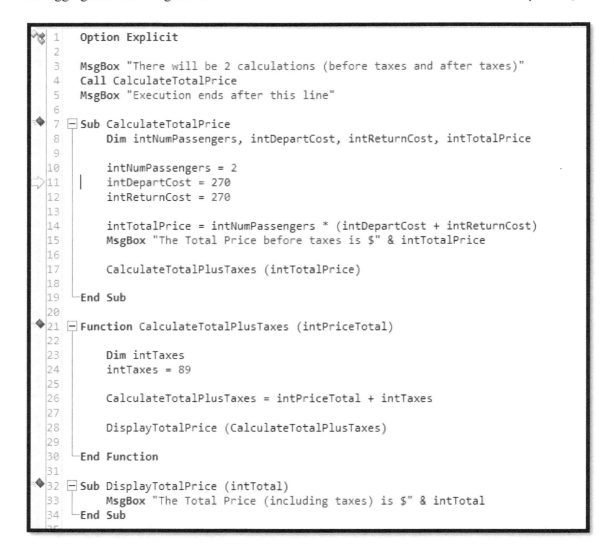

```
1     Option Explicit
2
3     MsgBox "There will be 2 calculations (before taxes and after taxes)"
4     Call CalculateTotalPrice
5     MsgBox "Execution ends after this line"
6
7   ⊟ Sub CalculateTotalPrice
8         Dim intNumPassengers, intDepartCost, intReturnCost, intTotalPrice
9
10        intNumPassengers = 2
11        intDepartCost = 270
12        intReturnCost = 270
13
14        intTotalPrice = intNumPassengers * (intDepartCost + intReturnCost)
15        MsgBox "The Total Price before taxes is $" & intTotalPrice
16
17        CalculateTotalPlusTaxes (intTotalPrice)
18
19    └ End Sub
20
21  ⊟ Function CalculateTotalPlusTaxes (intPriceTotal)
22
23        Dim intTaxes
24        intTaxes = 89
25
26        CalculateTotalPlusTaxes = intPriceTotal + intTaxes
27
28        DisplayTotalPrice (CalculateTotalPlusTaxes)
29
30    └ End Function
31
32  ⊟ Sub DisplayTotalPrice (intTotal)
33        MsgBox "The Total Price (including taxes) is $" & intTotal
34    └ End Sub
```

Explanation of the Step Over Command via Screenshots (Second Scenario)

o   The first screenshot displays, an execution that begins by using the Step Into which
    pauses at Line 3.

Skype: rex.jones34
Twitter: @RexJonesII
Email: Rex.Jones@Test4Success.org
LinkedIn: https://www.linkedin.com/in/rexjones34

Chapter 6
Debugging and Handling Errors   You Must Learn VBScript for QTP/UFT

Note: The Step Over command becomes available after pausing at line 3.

- o The second screenshot displays, "There will be 2 calculations (before taxes and after taxes)." This screenshot appears after stepping through line 3 which is a message box via Step Over or Step Into command.

- o The third screenshot pauses at line 4.
- o The fourth screenshot pauses at line 10 due to a procedure call "Call CalculateTotalPrice" after stepping through line 4 via Step Into command.
   Note: The Step Over command would have stepped over the procedure call "Call CalculateTotalPrice."

- o The fifth screenshot pauses at line 11 after stepping through line 10 via Step Over command.

The Step Over command operates like the Step Into command by executing only the current code line except when calling a procedure.

View the Call Stack

The Call Stack feature is a hierarchical list that keeps track of which procedures call one another. An automation engineer can view the hierarchical list to trace the execution path of procedures. The following is an example of the Call Stack feature:

3 Tips To Master QTP/UFT Within 30 Days
http://tinyurl.com/3-Tips-For-QTP-UFT

Free Webinars, Videos, and Live Trainings
http://tinyurl.com/Free-QTP-UFT-Selenium

Figure 6.18 – Screenshot of Call Stack

```
1    Option Explicit
2
3    MsgBox "There will be 2 calculations (before taxes and after taxes)"
4    Call CalculateTotalPrice
5    MsgBox "Execution ends after this line"
6
7  ⊟ Sub CalculateTotalPrice
8        Dim intNumPassengers, intDepartCost, intReturnCost, intTotalPrice
9
10       intNumPassengers = 2
11       intDepartCost = 270
12       intReturnCost = 270
13
14       intTotalPrice = intNumPassengers * (intDepartCost + intReturnCost)
15       MsgBox "The Total Price before taxes is $" & intTotalPrice
16
17       CalculateTotalPlusTaxes (intTotalPrice)
18
19   └ End Sub
20
21 ⊟ Function CalculateTotalPlusTaxes (intPriceTotal)
22
23       Dim intTaxes
24       intTaxes = 89
25
26       CalculateTotalPlusTaxes = intPriceTotal + intTaxes
27
28       DisplayTotalPrice (CalculateTotalPlusTaxes)
29
30   └ End Function
31
32 ⊟ Sub DisplayTotalPrice (intTotal)
33 │     MsgBox "The Total Price (including taxes) is $" & intTotal
34   └ End Sub
35
36
```

Call Stack ⟵	
Function name	**Line #**
→ DisplayTotalPrice	33
CalculateTotalPlusTaxes	28
CalculateTotalPrice	17
VBScript global code	4

The Call Stack reads from the bottom up, meaning the first procedure is located at the bottom of the Call Stack. This feature is valuable when dealing with programs that involve a procedure calling another procedure. The following explains the Call Stack window and procedure calls:

- o Function name "VBScript global code" begins the execution path. Line 4 is the location which calls procedure "CalculateTotalPrice."
- o Function name "CalculateTotalPrice" continues the execution path. Line 17 is the location which calls procedure "CalculateTotalPlusTax."
- o Function name "CalculateTotalPlusTax" continues the execution path. Line 28 is the location which calls procedure "DisplayTotalPrice."
- o Function name "DisplayTotalPrice" displays line 33 which is the current execution location.

Error-Handling

Error-handling introduces the process of responding to an error and how to prevent an error. Well-written programs include error-handling code that will stop execution of a program or continue executing the program in spite of errors. Handling errors in advance is a proactive technique consisting of the following two elements:

1. Err Object
2. On Error Statements

Err Object

The Err object is an intrinsic object with global scope that contains information about runtime errors. Intrinsic means the object does not need to be declared with a variable to hold the Err object. In addition, there is no reason to instantiate/create the object using CreateObject or New.

In memory, there is only one Err object at any given time. The Err object remains available with no information if no error occurred. However, if an error occurs, the Err object holds information about the last error. The following is a list of Err object properties and methods:

Figure 6.19 – Err Object Properties and Methods

Properties	Methods
Description	Clear
HelpContext	Raise
HelpFile	
Number	
Source	

Properties

Properties of the Err object stores information about runtime errors. The following are five Err object properties:

1. Description
2. HelpContext
3. HelpFile
4. Number
5. Source

Description

The Description property returns or sets a string containing a description of the error. A zero-length string is the default, unless the property is set or generated by an error. The following is the syntax of the Description property:

Syntax
Object.Description [= String]

Figure 6.20 – Description Property Syntax Details

Argument	Description

Object	Always the Err object
String	A string containing a description of the error

HelpContext

The HelpContext property sets or returns the help context value. This property is used to automatically display the specified Help topic in the HelpFile property. The following is the syntax of the HelpContext property:

Syntax
Object.HelpContext [= ContextID]

Figure 6.21 – HelpContext Property Syntax Details

Argument	Description
Object	Always the Err object
ContextID	An identifier for a help topic within the Help file

HelpFile

The HelpFile property sets or returns the path to a Help file. Normally, the HelpFile property is used with the HelpContext property. The following is the syntax of the HelpFile property:

Syntax
Object.HelpFile [= FilePath]

Figure 6.22 – HelpFile Property Syntax Details

Argument	Description
Object	Always the Err object
PathFile	Path to the Help file

Number

The Number property sets or returns a numeric value defining an error. This property is the Err object's default property. The following is the syntax of the Number property:

Syntax
Object.Number [= ErrorNumber]

Figure 6.23 – Number Property Syntax Details

Argument	Description
Object	Always the Err object
ErrorNumber	An integer representing a VBScript error or an SCODE error value

Source

The Source property sets or returns the name of the application or object that reported the error. Usually, the source is the class name or Program ID (ProgID) of the object generating an error. The following is the syntax for the Source property:

Syntax
Object.Source [= String]

Figure 6.24 – Source Property Syntax Details

Argument	Description
Object	Always the Err object
String	A string representing the application that generated the error

Methods

Methods of the Err objects allows an error to be raised or cleared. The following are two Err object methods:

1. Clear
2. Raise

Skype: rex.jones34
Twitter: @RexJonesII
Email: Rex.Jones@Test4Success.org
LinkedIn: https://www.linkedin.com/in/rexjones34

Clear

The Clear method resets all of the properties of the Err object to zero or zero-length string. Ideally, the Err object is reset after every error to avoid the mistake of dealing with the same error multiple times. The following is the syntax of the Clear method:

Syntax

Object.Clear

Figure 6.25 – Clear Method Syntax Details

Argument	Description
Object	Always the Err object

Raise

The Raise method generates a runtime error. Raising errors can change an error into another error, so that the error can be handled. The following is the syntax of the Raise method:

Syntax

Object.Raise (Number, Source, Description, HelpFile, HelpContext)

Figure 6.26 – Raise Method Syntax Details

Argument	Description
Object	Always the Err object
Number	Identifies the error
Source	Identifies the name of the object or application
Description	Description of the error
HelpFile	Path to the help file
HelpContext	Context ID identifying a topic within the help file

On Error Statements

On Error statements are features of VBScript that regulates the error control program settings. Regulation involves enabling or disabling the error-handling process. There are two On Error component statements:

o   On Error Resume Next
o   On Error GoTo 0

On Error Resume Next

The On Error Resume Next statement forces execution to continue following the statement that caused the runtime error. This statement turns the error control to Off which means VBScript ignores a particular error and continues executing the program. The following is an On Error Resume Next example:

Figure 6.27 – Screenshot of Sample Code

```
1    Option Explicit
2
3    On Error Resume Next
4
5    Dim intAvgPrice
6
7    intAvgPrice = 100/0
8
9    MsgBox "The average price per passenger is $" & intAvgPrice
10
```

Option Explicit

On Error Resume Next

Dim intAvgPrice

intAvgPrice = 100/0

MsgBox "The average price per passenger is $" & intAvgPrice

The output displays, "The average price per passenger is $."

Figure 6.28 – Screenshot Displaying Output from Above Code

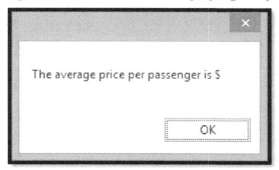

A runtime error did not occur after executing line 7: "intAvgPrice = 100/0." However, the error was ignored and execution continued to line 9, which displayed an empty value for intAvgPrice. Code from Figure 6.3 displayed a Run Error while mistakenly trying to divide by zero:

Note: Automation engineers must be careful when suppressing errors using the On Error Resume Next statement. It is best to use the On Error Resume Next with the On Error GoTo 0 statement.

On Error GoTo 0
The On Error GoTo 0 statement turns the error control to On. As a general rule, both statements (On Error Resume Next and On Error GoTo 0) should always be used together. Automation engineers utilize both statements together to set traps for errors. There are times when an automation engineer knows an error may occur in a specific part of their code. For

instance, the Application Under Test (AUT) or database can possibly return bad data. The following is an example of the On Error Resume Next and On Error GoTo 0 statements:

Figure 6.29 – Screenshot of Sample Code

```
1   Option Explicit
2
3   Dim intNumPassengers, intDepartCost, intReturnCost, intTotalBeforeTaxes, intAvgPrice
4
5   On Error Resume Next
6       'Demonstration purposes, the value for intNumPassengers returned from the AUT
7       intNumPassengers = 0
8       intDepartCost = 270
9       intReturnCost = 270
10
11      intTotalBeforeTaxes = intDepartCost + intReturnCost
12      intAvgPrice = intTotalBeforeTaxes / intNumPassengers
13
14      If Err.Number = 0 Then
15          MsgBox "The average flight price is $" & intAvgPrice
16      Else
17          MsgBox "Bad data returned from the Application Under Test (AUT)"
18      End If
19
20  On Error GoTo 0
```

Option Explicit

Dim intNumPassengers, intDepartCost, intReturnCost, intTotalBeforeTaxes, intAvgPrice

On Error Resume Next
   'Demonstration purposes, the value for intNumPassengers returned from the AUT
   intNumPassengers = 0
   intDepartCost = 270
   intReturnCost = 270

   intTotalBeforeTaxes = intDepartCost + intReturnCost
   intAvgPrice = intTotalBeforeTaxes / intNumPassengers

Skype: rex.jones34
Twitter: @RexJonesII
Email: Rex.Jones@Test4Success.org
LinkedIn: https://www.linkedin.com/in/rexjones34

If Err.Number = 0 **Then**
   MsgBox "The average flight price is $" & intAvgPrice
Else
   MsgBox "Bad data returned from the Application Under Test (AUT)"
End If

On Error GoTo 0

The output displays, "Bad data returned from the Application Under Test (AUT)."

Figure 6.30 – Screenshot Displaying Output from Above Code

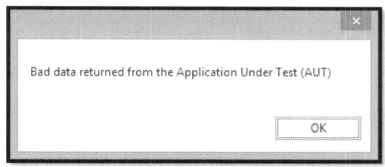

An error trap was set at line 12 in order to catch the bad data from line 7: "intNumPassengers = 0." However, the On Error Resume Next statement turns the error control to Off, so the error is not displayed while the On Error GoTo 0 statement turns the control back to On. Setting the error control to On, will display all errors after the On Error GoTo 0 statement.

Note: Code line 12 is similar to code line 5 from Figure 6.4, which results in a "Division by zero" error.

Chapter 6 covered the different types of errors, debugging, and how to handle errors. The three types of errors are syntax, runtime, and logical. Debugging is the process of finding and

3 Tips To Master QTP/UFT Within 30 Days
http://tinyurl.com/3-Tips-For-QTP-UFT

Free Webinars, Videos, and Live Trainings
http://tinyurl.com/Free-QTP-UFT-Selenium

fixing errors. Error-handling is the process of responding to an error. Chapter 7 will explain the Windows Script Host (WSH) which is a tool for establishing an environment for hosting scripts.

Chapter 7
Windows Script Host (WSH)

Windows Script Host (WSH) is an administration tool for Windows that establishes an environment for hosting scripts. A set of guidelines are provided by the WSH when scripts are executed. In addition, objects and services are made available via WSH for the scripts. Scripts are executed on two interfaces (CScript & WScript). CScript executes scripts on the command line while WScript executes scripts within the Windows environment. The following tasks can be accomplished when using objects and services:

- o   Retrieve and modify environment variables
- o   Map network drives
- o   Connect to printers
- o   Modify registry keys
- o   Access the current working directory
- o   Access and manipulate servers
- o   Run scripts remotely

This chapter describes the following about Windows Script Host (WSH):

- ✓   WSH Object Models
- ✓   WSH Properties
- ✓   WSH Methods

WSH Object Models

The WSH Object Model consists of the following 14 objects:

3 Tips To Master QTP/UFT Within 30 Days
http://tinyurl.com/3-Tips-For-QTP-UFT

Free Webinars, Videos, and Live Trainings
http://tinyurl.com/Free-QTP-UFT-Selenium

Figure 7.1 – WSH Object Models

WScript	WshRemoteError
WshArguments	WshShell
WshNamed	WshShortcut
WshUnnamed	WshSpecialFolders
WshNetwork	WshURLShortcut
WshController	WshEnvironment
WshRemote	WshScriptExec

Skype: rex.jones34
Twitter: @RexJonesII
Email: Rex.Jones@Test4Success.org
LinkedIn: https://www.linkedin.com/in/rexjones34

Chapter 7
Windows Script Host (WSH)   You Must Learn VBScript for QTP/UFT

Figure 7.2 - WSH Object Model Hierarchy

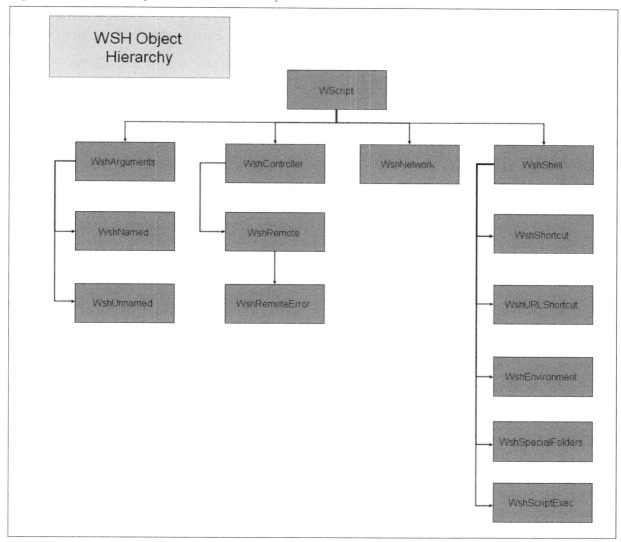

3 Tips To Master QTP/UFT Within 30 Days
http://tinyurl.com/3-Tips-For-QTP-UFT

Free Webinars, Videos, and Live Trainings
http://tinyurl.com/Free-QTP-UFT-Selenium

WScript Object

The WScript object is the root object of the Windows Script Host (WSH) object hierarchy. This object grants access to properties and methods that access a range of information. The WScript object has 12 properties and seven methods:

WScript Properties

The following properties are accessed by WScript object:

Figure 7.3 – WScript Properties

Arguments	ScriptFullName
BuildVersion	ScriptName
FullName (WScript)	StdErr
Interactive	StdIn
Name	StdOut
Path	Version

WScript Methods

The following methods are accessed by WScript object:

Figure 7.4 – WScript Methods

ConnectObject	GetObject
CreateObject	Quit
DisconnectObject	Sleep
Echo	

WshArguments Object

The WshArguments object grants access to the collection of command-line parameters. Each collection is returned by WScript object's Argument property. In addition, the WshArguments object create scripts to write reusable code. The WshArguments object has four properties and two methods:

Skype: rex.jones34
Twitter: @RexJonesII
Email: Rex.Jones@Test4Success.org
LinkedIn: https://www.linkedin.com/in/rexjones34

Chapter 7
Windows Script Host (WSH)   You Must Learn VBScript for QTP/UFT

WshArguments Properties

The following properties are accessed by WshArguments object:

Figure 7.5 – WshArguments Properties

Item	Named
Length	Unnamed

WshArguments Methods

The following methods are accessed by WshArguments object:

- o Count
- o ShowUsage

WshNamed Object

The WshNamed object grants access to the named arguments from the command line. A collection of arguments that have names is returned by the Named property of the WshArguments object. This collection uses the argument name as the index to retrieve individual argument values. The WshNamed object has two properties and two methods:

WshNamed Properties

The following properties are accessed by WshNamed object:

- o Item
- o Length

WshNamed Methods

The following methods are accessed by WshNamed object:

- o Count
- o Exists

3 Tips To Master QTP/UFT Within 30 Days
http://tinyurl.com/3-Tips-For-QTP-UFT

Free Webinars, Videos, and Live Trainings
http://tinyurl.com/Free-QTP-UFT-Selenium

WshUnnamed Object

The WshUnnamed object grants access to the unnamed arguments from the command line.
All individual argument values are retrieved from a collection using zero-based indexes. The
collection is a read-only collection that is returned by the Unnamed property of the
WshArguments object. The WshUnnamed object has two properties and one method:

WshUnnamed Properties
The following properties are accessed by WshUnnamed object:

- o Item
- o Length

WshUnnamed Method
The following method is accessed by WshUnnamed object:

- o Count

WshNetwork Object

The WshNetwork object grants access to resources shared on a network via a connected
computer. The WshNetwork object has three properties and eight methods:

WshNetwork Properties
The following properties are accessed by WshNetwork object:

- o ComputerName
- o UserDomain
- o UserName

WshNetwork Methods
The following methods are accessed by WshNetwork object:

Figure 7.6 – WshNetwork Methods

AddWindowsPrinterConnection	MapNetworkDrive

Skype: rex.jones34
Twitter: @RexJonesII
Email: Rex.Jones@Test4Success.org
LinkedIn: https://www.linkedin.com/in/rexjones34

AddPrinterConnection	RemoveNetworkDrive
EnumNetworkDrives	RemovePrinterConnection
EnumPrinterConnections	SetDefaultPrinter

WshController Object

The WshController object grants access to create a process for remote scripts. The WshController object has one method:

WshController Method

The following method is accessed by WshController object:

- o CreateScript

WshRemote Object

The WshRemote object grants access to the remote script process. This object permits computer systems on a network to be admitted via remote. The WshRemote object has two properties and one method:

WshRemote Properties

The following properties are accessed by WshRemote object:

- o Error
- o Status

WshRemote Method

The following method is accessed by WshRemote object:

- o Execute

3 Tips To Master QTP/UFT Within 30 Days
http://tinyurl.com/3-Tips-For-QTP-UFT

Free Webinars, Videos, and Live Trainings
http://tinyurl.com/Free-QTP-UFT-Selenium

WshRemoteError Object

The WshRemoteError object grants access to the error information. Errors are available when a remote script is terminated due to a script error. This object is returned by the Error property of WshRemote object. The WshRemoteError object has six properties:

WshRemoteError Properties

The following properties are accessed by WshRemoteError object:

- o Description
- o Line
- o Character
- o Number
- o SourceText
- o Source

WshShell Object

The WshShell object grants access to the native Windows shell. This object permits access to system environment variables, Windows special folders, create shortcuts, etc. The WshShell object has three properties and 11 methods:

WshShell Properties

The following properties are accessed by WshShell object:

- o CurrentDirectory
- o Environment
- o SpecialFolders

WshShell Methods

The following methods are accessed by WshShell object:

Figure 7.7 – WshShell Methods

AppActivate	RegDelete

Skype: rex.jones34
Twitter: @RexJonesII
Email: Rex.Jones@Test4Success.org
LinkedIn: https://www.linkedin.com/in/rexjones34

CreateShortcut	RegRead
Exec	RegWrite
ExpandEnvironmentStrings	Run
LogEvent	SendKeys
PopUp	

WshShortcut Object

The WshShortcut object permits a shortcut to be created programmatically. The WshShortcut object has nine properties and one method:

WshShortcut Properties
The following properties are accessed by WshShortcut object:

Figure 7.8 – WshShortcut Properties

Arguments	RelativePath
Description	TargetPath
FullName (WshShortcut)	WindowStyle
HotKey	WorkingDirectory
IconLocation	

WshShortcut Method
The following method is accessed by WshShortcut object:

o   Save

WshSpecialFolders Object

The WshSpecialFolders object grants access to a collection of special folders referenced by Windows. This object is returned by the SpecialFolders property of WshShell object. Moreover, the collection retrieves the paths to special folders utilizing the special folder

3 Tips To Master QTP/UFT Within 30 Days
http://tinyurl.com/3-Tips-For-QTP-UFT

Free Webinars, Videos, and Live Trainings
http://tinyurl.com/Free-QTP-UFT-Selenium

name as the index. Each path depends on the user's environment. The WshSpecialFolders object has two properties and one method:

WshSpecialFolders Properties
The following properties are accessed by WshSpecialFolders object:

- o Item
- o Length

WshSpecialFolders Method
The following method is accessed by WshSpecialFolders object:

- o Count

WshURLShortcut Object
The WshURLShortcut object permits an internet resource shortcut to be created programmatically. The WshURLShortcut object has two properties and one method:

WshURLShortcut Properties
The following properties are accessed by WshURLShortcut object:

- o FullName (WshURLShortcut)
- o TargetPath

WshURLShortcut Method
The following method is accessed by WshURLShortcut object:

- o Save

WshEnvironment Object
The WshEnvironment object grants access to a collection of environment variables referenced by Windows. This object is returned by the Environment property of WshShell object. Environment variables are retrieved individually from a collection by using the

Skype: rex.jones34
Twitter: @RexJonesII
Email: Rex.Jones@Test4Success.org
LinkedIn: https://www.linkedin.com/in/rexjones34

environment variable name as the index. The WshEnvironment object has two properties and two methods:

WshEnvironment Properties
The following properties are accessed by WshEnvironment object:

- o Item
- o Length (WshEnvironment)

WshEnvironment Methods
The following methods are accessed by WshEnvironment object:

- o Count
- o Remove

WshScriptExec Object
The WshScriptExec object supplies status information about a script. This object is returned by the Exec method of WshShell object. The WshScriptExec object has six properties and one method:

WshScriptExec Properties
The following properties are accessed by WshScriptExec object:

- o ExitCode
- o ProcessID
- o Status
- o StdErr
- o StdIn
- o StdOut

WshScriptExec Method
The following method is accessed by WshScriptExec object:

3 Tips To Master QTP/UFT Within 30 Days
http://tinyurl.com/3-Tips-For-QTP-UFT

Free Webinars, Videos, and Live Trainings
http://tinyurl.com/Free-QTP-UFT-Selenium

o Terminate

WSH Properties

The following is a list of Windows Script Host (WSH) properties:

Figure 7.9 WSH Properties

Arguments (WScript)	Line (WshRemoteError)
Arguments (WshShortcut)	Name (WScript)
AtEndOfLine	Named
AtEndOfStream	Number
BuildVersion	Path
Character	ProcessID
Column	RelativePath
ComputerName	ScriptFullName
CurrentDirectory	ScriptName
Description	Source
Description (WshRemoteError)	SourceText
Environment	SpecialFolders
Error (WshRemote)	Status (WshRemote)
ExitCode	Status (WshScriptExec)
FullName (WScript)	StdErr (WScript)
FullName (WshShortcut)	StdErr (WshScriptExec)
FullName (WshURLShortcut)	StdIn (WScript)
HotKey	StdIn (WshScriptExec)
IconLocation	StdOut (WScript)

Skype: rex.jones34
Twitter: @RexJonesII
Email: Rex.Jones@Test4Success.org
LinkedIn: https://www.linkedin.com/in/rexjones34

Interactive	StdOut (WshScriptExec)
Item	TargetPath
Item (WshNamed)	Unnamed
Item (WshUnnamed)	UserDomain
Length (WshArguments)	UserName
Length (WshEnvironment)	Version
Length (WshSpecialFolders)	WindowStyle
Line (WScript)	WorkingDirectory

Arguments Property (WScript)

The Arguments property (WScript) returns a collection of arguments via WshArguments object. This property utilizes a zero-based index to retrieve individual arguments. The following is the syntax for Arguments property (WScript):

Syntax
Object.Arguments

Figure 7.10 – Arguments Property (WScript) Syntax Details

Argument	**Description**
Object	Name of a WScript object

Arguments Property (WshShortcut)

The Arguments property (WshShortcut) sets the arguments for a shortcut or identifies a shortcut's arguments. The following is the syntax for Arguments property (WshShortcut):

Syntax
Object.Arguments

3 Tips To Master QTP/UFT Within 30 Days
http://tinyurl.com/3-Tips-For-QTP-UFT

Free Webinars, Videos, and Live Trainings
http://tinyurl.com/Free-QTP-UFT-Selenium

Figure 7.11 – Arguments Property (WshShortcut) Syntax Details

Argument	Description
Object	Name of a WshShortcut object

AtEndOfLine Property

The AtEndOfLine property returns a Boolean value specifying if the end of line in an input stream has been reached. True is returned if the stream pointer immediately precedes the end of line marker in an input stream. False is returned if the stream pointer does not immediately precedes the end of line marker in an input stream. The following is the syntax for AtEndOfLine property:

Syntax
Object.AtEndOfLine

Figure 7.12 – AtEndOfLine Property Syntax Details

Argument	Description
Object	StdIn text stream object

AtEndOfStream Property

The AtEndOfStream property returns a Boolean value specifying if the end of an input stream has been reached. True is returned if the stream pointer is at the end of an input stream. False is returned if the stream pointer is not at the end of an input stream. The following is the syntax for AtEndOfStream property:

Syntax
Object.AtEndOfStream

Figure 7.13 – AtEndOfStream Property Syntax Details

Argument	Description
Object	StdIn text stream object

Skype: rex.jones34
Twitter: @RexJonesII
Email: Rex.Jones@Test4Success.org
LinkedIn: https://www.linkedin.com/in/rexjones34

BuildVersion Property

The BuildVersion property is read-only and returns a value which is the build version number of the Windows Script Host. The following is the syntax for BuildVersion property:

Syntax
Object.BuildVersion

Figure 7.14 – BuildVersion Property Syntax Details

Argument	Description
Object	Name of a WScript object

Character Property

The Character property displays a specific character in a line of code that occupies an error. Each line starts the first character with position one. The following is the syntax for Character property:

Syntax
Object.Character

Figure 7.15 – Character Property Syntax Details

Argument	Description
Object	Name of a WshRemoteError object

Column Property

The Column property is read-only and returns the column number of the current character position in an input stream. This property equals to one after a newline character is written. The following is the syntax for Column property:

3 Tips To Master QTP/UFT Within 30 Days
http://tinyurl.com/3-Tips-For-QTP-UFT

Free Webinars, Videos, and Live Trainings
http://tinyurl.com/Free-QTP-UFT-Selenium

Syntax
Object.Column

Figure 7.16 – Column Property Syntax Details

Argument	Description
Object	StdIn text stream object

ComputerName Property
The ComputerName property is read-only and returns the computer system name. The following is the syntax for ComputerName property:

Syntax
Object.ComputerName

Figure 7.17 – ComputerName Property Syntax Details

Argument	Description
Object	Name of a WshNetwork object

CurrentDirectory Property
The CurrentDirectory property retrieves or changes the current active directory. A full path of the active process is returned. The following is the syntax for CurrentDirectory property:

Syntax
Object.CurrentDirectory

Figure 7.18 – CurrentDirectory Property Syntax Details

Argument	Description
Object	Name of a WshShell object

Skype: rex.jones34
Twitter: @RexJonesII
Email: Rex.Jones@Test4Success.org
LinkedIn: https://www.linkedin.com/in/rexjones34

Description Property

The Description property sets or retrieves a description of the shortcut. The following is the syntax for Description property:

Syntax

Object.Description

Figure 7.19 – Description Property Syntax Details

Argument	Description
Object	Name of a WshShortcut object

Description Property (WshRemoteError)

The Description property (WshRemoteError) holds a description of the error that forced the remote script to stop. The following is the syntax for Description property (WshRemoteError):

Syntax

Object.Description

Figure 7.20 – Description Property (WshRemoteError) Syntax Details

Argument	Description
Object	Name of a WshRemoteError object

Environment Property

The Environment property is read-only and returns a collection of environment variables via WshEnvironment object. The following is the syntax for Environment property:

Syntax

Object.Environment (Type)

3 Tips To Master QTP/UFT Within 30 Days
http://tinyurl.com/3-Tips-For-QTP-UFT

Free Webinars, Videos, and Live Trainings
http://tinyurl.com/Free-QTP-UFT-Selenium

Figure 7.21 – Environment Property Syntax Details

Argument	Description
Object	Name of a WshShell object
Type	Indicates the environment variable location

Error Property (WshRemote)

The Error property (WshRemote) returns the WshRemoteError object which contains information regarding the error that forced the remote script to stop. The following is the syntax for Error property (WshRemote):

Syntax
Object.Error

Figure 7.22 – Error Property (WshRemote) Syntax Details

Argument	Description
Object	Name of a WshRemote object

ExitCode Property

The ExitCode property returns the exit code set by a program run utilizing the Exec method. The following is the syntax for ExitCode property:

Syntax
Object.ExitCode

Figure 7.23 – ExitCode Property Syntax Details

Argument	Description
Object	Name of a WshScriptExec object

Skype: rex.jones34
Twitter: @RexJonesII
Email: Rex.Jones@Test4Success.org
LinkedIn: https://www.linkedin.com/in/rexjones34

FullName Property (WScript)

The FullName property (WScript) returns the full path of the host executable file. The following is the syntax for FullName property (WScript):

Syntax
Object.FullName

Figure 7.24 – FullName Property (WScript) Syntax Details

Argument	Description
Object	Name of a WScript object

FullName Property (WshShortcut)

The FullName property (WshShortcut) is read-only and returns the full path to the shortcut object's target. This property is the default property for WshShortcut object. The following is the syntax for FullName property (WshShortcut):

Syntax
Object.FullName

Figure 7.25 – FullName Property (WshShortcut) Syntax Details

Argument	Description
Object	Name of a WshShortcut object

FullName Property (WshURLShortcut)

The FullName property (WshURLShortcut) is read-only and returns the full path of the shortcut file. The following is the syntax for FullName property (WshURLShortcut):

Syntax
Object.FullName

3 Tips To Master QTP/UFT Within 30 Days
http://tinyurl.com/3-Tips-For-QTP-UFT

Free Webinars, Videos, and Live Trainings
http://tinyurl.com/Free-QTP-UFT-Selenium

Figure 7.26 – FullName Property (WshURLShortcut) Syntax Details

Argument	Description
Object	Name of a WshURLShortcut object

HotKey Property

The HotKey property sets or retrieves the hotkey combination for a shortcut. This property assigns a key combination to a shortcut or identifies the key combination assigned to a shortcut. The following is the syntax for HotKey property:

Syntax
Object.HotKey = KeyCombination

Figure 7.27 – HotKey Property Syntax Details

Argument	Description
Object	Name of a WshShortcut object
KeyCombination	String representing a key combination to assign to the shortcut: **KeyCombination Syntax**: [KeyModifier]KeyName KeyModifier = Any of the following (Alt+, CTRL+, Shift+, EXT+)

IconLocation Property

The IconLocation property sets or retrieves the location of the icon to represent the shortcut. This property assigns an icon to a shortcut or identifies the icon assigned to a shortcut. The following is the syntax for IconLocation property:

Syntax
Object.IconLocation = LocationOfIcon

Figure 7.28 – IconLocation Property Syntax Details

Argument	Description

Skype: rex.jones34
Twitter: @RexJonesII
Email: Rex.Jones@Test4Success.org
LinkedIn: https://www.linkedin.com/in/rexjones34

| Object | Name of a WshShortcut object |
| LocationOfIcon | String that locates the icon which is a full path and an index associated with the icon. |

Interactive Property

The Interactive property returns a Boolean value that sets or identifies the script mode. This property has two modes which are Interactive (default) and Batch. The Interactive mode provides user interaction where input and output is enabled from the WSH. However, the Batch mode does not support input and output from WSH. The following is the syntax for Interactive property:

Syntax
Object.Interactive

Figure 7.29 – Interactive Property Syntax Details

Argument	**Description**
Object	Name of a WScript object

Item Property

The Item property returns a specific item from a collection. The following is the syntax for Item property:

Syntax
Object.Item (Index)

Figure 7.30 – Item Property Syntax Details

Argument	**Description**
Object	Result of the EnumNetworkDrives or EnumPrinterConnections method Object returned by the Environment or SpecialFolders properties
Index	Item to retrieve

3 Tips To Master QTP/UFT Within 30 Days
http://tinyurl.com/3-Tips-For-QTP-UFT

Free Webinars, Videos, and Live Trainings
http://tinyurl.com/Free-QTP-UFT-Selenium

Item Property (WshNamed)

The Item property (WshNamed) grants access to items in the WshNamed object. The following is the syntax for Item property (WshNamed):

Syntax
Object.Item (Key)

Figure 7.31 – Item Property (WshNamed) Syntax Details

Argument	Description
Object	Name of a WshNamed object
Key	Name of the item that will be retrieved

Item Property (WshUnnamed)

The Item property (WshUnnamed) returns an item utilizing a zero-based index. The following is the syntax for Item property (WshUnnamed):

Syntax
Object.Item (Key)

Figure 7.32 – Item (WshUnnamed) Property Syntax Details

Argument	Description
Object	Name of a WshUnnamed object
Key	Collection or WshUnnamed object

Length Property (WshArguments)

The Length property (WshArguments) is read-only and returns the number of command line parameters associated with a script. A script is the number of items in an argument's collection. The following is the syntax for Length property (WshArguments):

Skype: rex.jones34
Twitter: @RexJonesII
Email: Rex.Jones@Test4Success.org
LinkedIn: https://www.linkedin.com/in/rexjones34

Syntax

Object.Length

Figure 7.33 – Length Property (WshArguments) Syntax Details

Argument	Description
Object	Argument collection object

Length Property (WshEnvironment)

The Length property (WshEnvironment) is read-only and returns the number of items in an environment collection. The following is the syntax for Length property (WshEnvironment):

Syntax

Object.Length

Figure 7.34 – Length Property (WshEnvironment) Syntax Details

Argument	Description
Object	Name of a WshEnvironment object

Length Property (WshSpecialFolders)

The Length property (WshSpecialFolders) is read-only and returns the number of Windows special folders on the local computer system. The following is the syntax for Length property (WshSpecialFolders):

Syntax

Object.Length

Figure 7.35 – Length Property (WshSpecialFolders) Syntax Details

Argument	Description
Object	Name of a WshSpecialFolders object

3 Tips To Master QTP/UFT Within 30 Days
http://tinyurl.com/3-Tips-For-QTP-UFT

Free Webinars, Videos, and Live Trainings
http://tinyurl.com/Free-QTP-UFT-Selenium

Line Property (WScript)

The Line property (WScript) is read-only and returns the current line number in an input stream. The following is the syntax for Line property (WScript):

Syntax
Object.Stream.Line

Figure 7.36 – Line Property (WScript) Syntax Details

Argument	Description
Object	Name of a WScript object
Stream	StdIn property

Line Property (WshRemoteError)

The Line property (WshRemoteError) identifies the line in a script that holds an error. The following is the syntax for Line property (WshRemoteError):

Syntax
Object.Line

Figure 7.37 – Line Property (WshRemoteError) Syntax Details

Argument	Description
Object	Name of a WshRemoteError object

Name Property (WScript)

The Name property (WScript) is read-only and returns the name of the Windows Script Host. The following is the syntax for Name property (WScript):

Syntax
Object.Name

Figure 7.38 – Name Property Syntax Details

Argument	Description

| Object | Name of a WScript object |

Named Property

The Named property returns the WshNamed object which is a collection of named arguments. The following is the syntax for Named property:

Syntax
Object.Named

Figure 7.39 – Named Property Syntax Details

Argument	Description
Object	Name of a WshArguments object

Number Property

The Number property displays the error number representing a script error. The following is the syntax for Number property:

Syntax
Object.Number

Figure 7.40 – Number Property Syntax Details

Argument	Description
Object	Name of a WshRemoteError object

Path Property

The Path property is read-only and returns the full path name of the directory containing the host executable file "WScript." The following is the syntax for Path property:

Syntax
Object.Path

Figure 7.41 – Path Property Syntax Details

Argument	Description
Object	Name of a WScript object

ProcessID Property

The ProcessID for a process initiated by the WshScriptExec object. The following is the syntax for ProcessID property:

Syntax
Object.ProcessID

Figure 7.42 – ProcessID Property Syntax Details

Argument	Description
Object	Name of a WshScriptExec object

RelativePath Property

The RelativePath property assigns a relative path to a shortcut or identifies the relative path of a shortcut. The following is the syntax for RelativePath property:

Syntax
Object.RelativePath

Figure 7.43 – RelativePath Property Syntax Details

Argument	Description
Object	Name of a WshShortcut object

Skype: rex.jones34
Twitter: @RexJonesII
Email: Rex.Jones@Test4Success.org
LinkedIn: https://www.linkedin.com/in/rexjones34

ScriptFullName Property

The ScriptFullName property is read-only and returns the full path of the currently executing script. The following is the syntax for ScriptFullName property:

Syntax
Object.ScriptFullName

Figure 7.44 – ScriptFullName Property Syntax Details

Argument	Description
Object	Name of a WScript object

ScriptName Property

The ScriptName property is read-only and returns the file name of the currently executing script. The following is the syntax for ScriptName property:

Syntax
Object.ScriptName

Figure 7.45 – ScriptName Property Syntax Details

Argument	Description
Object	Name of a WScript object

Source Property

The Source property identifies the Component Object Model (COM) object responsible for forcing the script error. The following is the syntax for Source property:

Syntax
Object.Source

3 Tips To Master QTP/UFT Within 30 Days
http://tinyurl.com/3-Tips-For-QTP-UFT

Free Webinars, Videos, and Live Trainings
http://tinyurl.com/Free-QTP-UFT-Selenium

Figure 7.46 – Source Property Syntax Details

Argument	Description
Object	Name of a WshRemoteError object

SourceText Property

The SourceText property contains the line of source code that forced an error. The following is the syntax for SourceText property:

Syntax
Object.SourceText

Figure 7.47 – SourceText Property Syntax Details

Argument	Description
Object	Name of a WshRemoteError object

SpecialFolders Property

The SpecialFolders property is read-only and returns a collection of special folders via WshSpecialFolders object. The following is the syntax for SpecialFolders property:

Syntax
Object.SpecialFolders (SpecialFolderName)

Figure 7.48 – SpecialFolders Property Syntax Details

Argument	Description
Object	Name of a WshShell object
SpecialFolderName	Name of the special folder

Status Property (WshRemote)

The Status property (WshRemote) is read-only and displays the current status of the remote script. The following is the syntax for Status property (WshRemote):

Skype: rex.jones34
Twitter: @RexJonesII
Email: Rex.Jones@Test4Success.org
LinkedIn: https://www.linkedin.com/in/rexjones34

Syntax

Object.Status

Figure 7.49 – Status Property (WshRemote) Syntax Details

Argument	Description
Object	Name of a WshRemote object

The following are Status property (WshRemote) return values from an enumerated type:

Figure 7.50 - Status Property (WshRemote) Return Values

Return Value	Numeric Value	Description
NoTask	0	The remote script object has been created but has not yet executed
Running	1	The remote script object is currently running
Finished	2	The remote script object has finished running

Status Property (WshScriptExec)

The Status property (WshScriptExec) grants status information about a script run with the Exec method. The following is the syntax for Status property (WshScriptExec):

Syntax

Object.Status

Figure 7.51 – Status Property (WshScriptExec) Syntax Details

Argument	Description
Object	Name of a WshScriptExec object

The following are Status property (WshScriptExec) return values from an enumerated type:

Figure 7.52 – Status Property (WshScriptExec) Return Values

Value	Description
WshRunning (= 0)	Job is running
WshFinished (= 1)	Job has completed

StdErr Property (WScript)

The StdErr property (WScript) returns a write-only TextStream object that sends information to the Standard Error stream for the current script. The following is the syntax for StdErr property (WScript):

Syntax
Object.StdErr

Figure 7.53 – StdErr Property (WScript) Syntax Details

Argument	Description
Object	Name of a WScript object

Note: The StdErr property is read-only and can only be accessed while utilizing CScript. An error occurs if there is an attempt to access StdErr property via WScript.

StdErr Property (WshScriptExec)

The StdErr property (WshScriptExec) grants access to the StdErr output stream of WshScriptExec object. This property is used to retrieve data sent to the StdErr stream from a process initiated by the Exec method. The following is the syntax for StdErr property (WshScriptExec):

Syntax
Object.StdErr

Figure 7.54 – StdErr Property (WshScriptExec) Syntax Details

Argument	Description

Skype: rex.jones34
Twitter: @RexJonesII
Email: Rex.Jones@Test4Success.org
LinkedIn: https://www.linkedin.com/in/rexjones34

Object	Name of a WshScriptExec object

StdIn Property (WScript)

The StdIn property (WScript) returns a read-only TextStream object that reads information from the Standard Input stream for the current script. The following is the syntax for StdIn property (WScript):

Syntax
Object.StdIn

Figure 7.55 – StdIn Property (WScript) Syntax Details

Argument	Description
Object	Name of a WScript object

Note: The StdIn property is read-only and can only be accessed while utilizing CScript. An error occurs if there is an attempt to access the StdIn property via WScript.

StdIn Property (WshScriptExec)

The StdIn property (WshScriptExec) returns the StdIn input stream of the WshScriptExec object. This property is used to pass data sent to a process initiated by the Exec method. The following is the syntax for StdIn property (WshScriptExec):

Syntax
Object.StdIn

Figure 7.56 – StdIn Property (WshScriptExec) Syntax Details

Argument	Description
Object	Name of a WshScriptExec object

StdOut Property (WScript)

The StdOut property (WScript) returns a write-only TextStream object that sends information to the Standard Output stream for the current script. The following is the syntax for StdOut property (WScript):

Syntax
Object.StdOut

Figure 7.57 – StdOut Property (WScript) Syntax Details

Argument	Description
Object	Name of a WScript object

Note: The StdErr property is read-only and can only be accessed while utilizing CScript. An error occurs if there is an attempt to access StdErr property via WScript.

StdOut Property (WshScriptExec)

The StdOut property (WshScriptExec) returns the write-only StdOut output stream of the WshScriptExec object. This property holds information that is read-only which may be sent to the standard output. The following is the syntax for StdOut property (WshScriptExec):

Syntax
Object.StdOut

Figure 7.58 – StdOut Property (WshScriptExec) Syntax Details

Argument	Description
Object	Name of a WshScriptExec object

TargetPath Property

The TargetPath property is the target URL string of the WshURLShortcut object (shortcut's executable). The following is the syntax for TargetPath property:

Skype: rex.jones34
Twitter: @RexJonesII
Email: Rex.Jones@Test4Success.org
LinkedIn: https://www.linkedin.com/in/rexjones34

Syntax
Object.TargetPath

Figure 7.59 – TargetPath Property Syntax Details

Argument	Description
Object	Name of a WshShortcut or WshURLShortcut object

Unnamed Property

The Unnamed property returns the WshUnnamed object which is a collection of unnamed arguments. The following is the syntax for Unnamed property:

Syntax
Object.Unnamed

Figure 7.60 – Unnamed Property Syntax Details

Argument	Description
Object	Name of a WshArguments object

UserDomain Property

The UserDomain property is read-only and returns the current user's domain name. The following is the syntax for UserDomain property:

Syntax
Object.UserDomain

Figure 7.61 – UserDomain Property Syntax Details

Argument	Description
Object	Name of a WshNetwork object

UserName Property

The UserName property is read-only and returns the current user's name. The following is the syntax for UserName property:

Syntax
Object.UserName

Figure 7.62 – UserName Property Syntax Details

Argument	Description
Object	Name of a WshNetwork object

Version Property

The Version property is read-only and returns the version number of the Windows Script Host. The following is the syntax for Version property:

Syntax
Object.Version

Figure 7.63 – Version Property Syntax Details

Argument	Description
Object	Name of a WScript object

WindowStyle Property

The WindowStyle property assigns a window style to a shortcut or identifies the window style type used by the shortcut. The following is the syntax for WindowStyle property:

Syntax
Object.WindowStyle (StyleOfWindow)

Figure 7.64 – WindowStyle Property Syntax Details

Argument	Description

Skype: rex.jones34
Twitter: @RexJonesII
Email: Rex.Jones@Test4Success.org
LinkedIn: https://www.linkedin.com/in/rexjones34

Object	Name of a WshShortcut object
StyleOfWindow	Sets the window style

The following settings are available for the StyleOfWindow argument:

Figure 7.65 – Window Style Settings

StyleOfWindow	Description
1	Activates and displays a window
3	Activates the window and displays it as a maximized window
7	Minimizes the window and activates the next top-level window

WorkingDirectory Property

The WorkingDirectory property sets or retrieves the default working directory. This property assigns a working directory to a shortcut or identifies the working directory utilized by a shortcut. The following is the syntax for WorkingDirectory property:

Syntax
Object.WorkingDirectory (Directory)

Figure 7.66 – WorkingDirectory Property Syntax Details

Argument	Description
Object	Name of a WshShortcut object
Directory	Directory where the shortcut starts

WSH Methods

The following is a list of Windows Script Host (WSH) Methods:

3 Tips To Master QTP/UFT Within 30 Days
http://tinyurl.com/3-Tips-For-QTP-UFT

Free Webinars, Videos, and Live Trainings
http://tinyurl.com/Free-QTP-UFT-Selenium

Figure 7.67 WSH Methods

AddPrinterConnection	ReadAll
AddWindowsPrinterConnection	ReadLine
AppActivate	RegDelete
Close	RegRead
ConnectObject	RegWrite
Count	Remove
CreateObject	RemoveNetworkDrive
CreateScript	RemovePrinterConnection
CreateShortcut	Run
DisconnectObject	Save
Echo	SendKeys
EnumNetworkDrives	SetDefaultPrinter
EnumPrinterConnections	ShowUsage
Exec	Sign
Execute	SignFile
Exists	Skip
ExpandEnvironmentStrings	SkipLine
GetObject	Sleep
GetResource	Terminate (WshScriptExec)
LogEvent	Verify
MapNetworkDrive	VerifyFile
PopUp	Write
Quit	WriteBlankLines
Read	WriteLine

AddPrinterConnection Method

The AddPrinterConnection method adds a connection from a computer to a remote printer. The following is the syntax for AddPrinterConnection method:

Skype: rex.jones34
Twitter: @RexJonesII
Email: Rex.Jones@Test4Success.org
LinkedIn: https://www.linkedin.com/in/rexjones34

Syntax

Object.AddPrinterConnection (LocalName, RemoteName [, UpdateProfile] [, User]
[Password])

Figure 7.68 – AddPrinterConnection Method Syntax Details

Argument	Description
Object	Name of a WshNetwork object
LocalName	Value specifying the local name to assign to the connected printer
RemoteName	Value specifying the remote printer name
UpdateProfile	Boolean value specifying if the printer mapping is stored in the current user's profile. True: Mapping is saved to the current user's profile False: (Default) Mapping is not saved to the current user's profile
User	Value specifying the user's name. If mapping a remote printer using the profile of someone else then the User and Password credentials can be supplied
Password	Value specifying the user's password. If mapping a remote printer using the profile of someone else then the User and Password credentials can be supplied

AddWindowsPrinterConnection Method

The AddWindowsPrinterConnection method adds a connection from a computer to a
Windows-based printer. The following is the syntax for AddWindowsPrinterConnection
method:

Syntax

Object.AddWindowsPrinterConnection (PrinterPath, DriverName [, Port])

Figure 7.69 – AddWindowsPrinterConnection Method Syntax Details

Argument	Description
Object	Name of a WshNetwork object

PrinterPath	Value specifying the printer connection path
DriverName	Value specifying the driver name
Port	Value specifying a printer port for the printer connection

AppActivate Method

The AppActivate method activates an application window. This method changes the focus to the named window or application. The following is the syntax for AppActivate method:

Syntax
Object.AppActivate (Title)

Figure 7.70 – AppActivate Method Syntax Details

Argument	Description
Object	Name of a WshShell object
Title	Specifies the application to activate

Close Method

The Close method closes a text stream. The following is the syntax for Close method:

Syntax
Object.Close

Figure 7.71 – Close Method Syntax Details

Argument	Description
Object	StdIn, StdOut, or StdErr text stream objects

Note: The StdIn, StdOut, and StdErr properties and methods work when accessed while utilizing CScript. However, an error occurs if accessed by WScript.

Chapter 7
Windows Script Host (WSH)   You Must Learn VBScript for QTP/UFT

ConnectObject Method

The ConnectObject method connects the events of an object to functions with a particular prefix in the currently executing script. The following is the syntax for ConnectObject method:

Syntax
Object.ConnectObject (ObjectEventSource, SubPrefix)

Figure 7.72 – ConnectObject Method Syntax Details

Argument	Description
Object	Name of a WScript object
ObjectEventSource	Object that connects to event handlers
SubPrefix	String that is joined to the event name

Count Method

The Count method returns the number of components in an object. The following is the syntax for Count method:

Syntax
Object.Count

Figure 7.73 – Count Method Syntax Details

Argument	Description
Object	Name of a WshArguments, WshEnvironment, WshNamed, WshUnnamed, or WshSpecialFolders object
	Name of Arguments property of WScript

CreateObject Method

The CreateObject method creates a Component Object Model (COM) object. An object created with the CreateObject method using SubPrefix argument is a connected object. However, the ConnectObject method must be used if an object is created without using the SubPrefix argument. The following is the syntax for ConnectObject method:

Syntax
Object.CreateObject (ProgID, SubPrefix)

Figure 7.74 – ConnectObject Method Syntax Details

Argument	Description
Object	Name of a WScript object
ProgID	Value of the programmatic identifier that will be assigned to the created object
SubPrefix	Value of the function prefix

CreateScript Method

The CreateScript method creates a WshRemote object. The following is the syntax for CreateScript method:

Syntax
Object.CreateScript (CommandLine, [MachineName])

Figure 7.75 – CreateScript Method Syntax Details

Argument	Description
Object	Name of a WshController object
CommandLine	Value specifying the script's path
MachineName	Value specifying the remote computer system name

Skype: rex.jones34
Twitter: @RexJonesII
Email: Rex.Jones@Test4Success.org
LinkedIn: https://www.linkedin.com/in/rexjones34

CreateShortcut Method

The CreateShortcut method creates and returns a WshShortcut object or a WshURLShortcut object. A new shortcut is created or an existing shortcut is opened. The following is the syntax for CreateShortcut method:

Syntax

Object.CreateShortcut (PathName)

Figure 7.76 – CreateShortcut Method Syntax Details

Argument	Description
Object	Name of a WshShell object
PathName	Value specifying the pathname of the shortcut that will be created

DisconnectObject Method

The DisconnectObject method disconnects a connection between an object's event sources (currently executing script and specified object). The following is the syntax for DisconnectObject method:

Syntax

Object.DisconnectObject (Obj)

Figure 7.77 – DisconnectObject Method Syntax Details

Argument	Description
Object	Name of a WScript object
Obj	Value of the object to disconnect

Echo Method

The Echo method sends information to a message box (WScript) or command console (CScript) window. The following is the syntax for Echo method:

3 Tips To Master QTP/UFT Within 30 Days
http://tinyurl.com/3-Tips-For-QTP-UFT

Free Webinars, Videos, and Live Trainings
http://tinyurl.com/Free-QTP-UFT-Selenium

Syntax
Object.Echo [Arg1] [,Arg2] [,Arg3] …

Figure 7.78 – Echo Method Syntax Details

Argument	Description
Object	Name of a WScript object
Arg1, Arg2, Arg3	Value of item(s) that will be displayed

EnumNetworkDrives Method

The EnumNetworkDrives method returns a collection of the current network drive mapping information. Index zero (0) is the first item in the collection. Even-numbered items in the collection serve as local names of logical drives. Odd-numbered items serve as the associated Universal Naming Convention (UNC) share names. The following is the syntax for EnumNetworkDrives method:

Syntax
Object.EnumNetworkDrives

Figure 7.79 – EnumNetworkDrives Method Syntax Details

Argument	Description
Object	Name of a WshNetwork object

EnumPrinterConnections Method

The EnumPrinterConnections method returns a collection of the current network printer mapping information. Index zero (0) is the first item in the collection. Even-numbered items in the collection serve as printer ports. Odd-numbered items serve as the networked printer Universal Naming Convention (UNC) names. The following is the syntax for EnumPrinterConnections method:

Syntax
Object.EnumPrinterConnections

Figure 7.80 – EnumPrinterConnections Method Syntax Details

Argument	Description
Object	Name of a WshNetwork object

Exec Method

The Exec method runs an application in a child command-shell, providing access to the StdIn, StdOut, StdErr streams. This method returns a WshScriptExec object, which provides status and error information. The following is the syntax for Exec method:

Syntax
Object.Exec (Command)

Figure 7.81 – Exec Method Syntax Details

Argument	Description
Object	Name of a WshShell object
Command	Value specifying the command line used to run the script

Execute Method

The Execute method starts an execution of a remote script object. The following is the syntax for Execute method:

Syntax
Object.Execute

Figure 7.82 – Execute Method Syntax Details

Argument	Description
Object	Name of a WshRemote object

3 Tips To Master QTP/UFT Within 30 Days
http://tinyurl.com/3-Tips-For-QTP-UFT

Free Webinars, Videos, and Live Trainings
http://tinyurl.com/Free-QTP-UFT-Selenium

Exists Method

The Exists method indicates if a specific key value exists in the WshNamed object. This method returns a Boolean value. True is returned if the requested argument was specified on the command line. However, False is returned if the requested argument was not specified on the command line. The following is the syntax for Exists method:

Syntax
Object.Exists (Key)

Figure 7.83 – Exists Method Syntax Details

Argument	Description
Object	Name of a WshNamed object
Key	Value specifying an argument of the WshNamed object

ExpandEnvironmentStrings Method

The ExpandEnvironmentStrings method expands the environment variables in a string and returns an environment variable's expanded value. The following is the syntax for ExpandEnvironmentStrings method:

Syntax
Object.ExpandEnvironmentStrings (EnvironmentVariableString)

Figure 7.84 – ExpandEnvironmentStrings Method Syntax Details

Argument	Description
Object	Name of a WshShell object
EnvironmentVariableString	Value specifying the environment variable name that will be expanded

GetObject Method

The GetObject method retrieves an existing object or creates a new object from a file. Each file loads into an application and returns a reference to the application object. The following is the syntax for GetObject method:

Syntax
Object.GetObject (PathName [,ProgID] [,SubPrefix])

Figure 7.85 – GetObject Method Syntax Details

Argument	Description
Object	Name of a WScript object
PathName	Location of the file that will be loaded into the application
ProgID	An object's programmatic identifier
SubPrefix	Utilized to synchronize the object's events.

GetResource Method

The GetResource method returns the value of a resource defined with the <resource> element. A resource element is used to isolate strings or numbers that are within the WSH script (.wsf) file. The following is the syntax for GetResource method:

Syntax
GetResource (ResourceID)

Figure 7.86 – GetResource Method Syntax Details

Argument	Description
ResourceID	Identifies the resource information contained within a set of resource tags in an *.WSF script file

LogEvent Method

The LogEvent method adds an event entry to a log file and returns a Boolean value. The following is the syntax for LogEvent method:

Syntax
Object.LogEvent (Type, Message [,Target])

Figure 7.87 – LogEvent Method Syntax Details

Argument	Description
Object	Name of a WshNetwork object
Type	Value that serve as the event type
Message	Value containing the log entry text
Target	Value specifying computer system name where the log entry is stored

The following is the six event types:

Figure 7.88 – Event Types

Type	Value
0	SUCCESS
1	ERROR
2	WARNING
4	INFORMATION
8	AUDIT_SUCCESS
16	AUDIT_FAILURE

MapNetworkDrive Method

The MapNetworkDrive method adds (also known as maps) a shared network drive onto the local drive letter (computer system). The following is the syntax for MapNetworkDrive method:

Skype: rex.jones34
Twitter: @RexJonesII
Email: Rex.Jones@Test4Success.org
LinkedIn: https://www.linkedin.com/in/rexjones34

Syntax

Object.MapNetworkDrive (LocalName, RemoteName, [UpdateProfile], [User], [Password])

Figure 7.89 – MapNetworkDrive Method Syntax Details

Argument	Description
Object	Name of a WshNetwork object
LocalName	Value specifying the local name
RemoteName	Value specifying the share's UNC name
UpdateProfile	Boolean value specifying if the mapping information is stored in the current user's profile. True: Mapping is stored in the user's profile False: (Default) Mapping is not stored in the user's profile
User	Value specifying the user's name. If mapping a network drive using the profile of someone else then the User and Password credentials must be supplied
Password	Value specifying the user's password. If mapping a network drive using the profile of someone else then the User and Password credentials must be supplied

PopUp Method

The PopUp method displays information in a pop-up message box. The following is the syntax for PopUp method:

Syntax

Object.PopUp

Figure 7.90 – PopUp Method Syntax Details

Argument	Description
Object	Name of a WshShell object
Text	Value specifying the text that will appear in the pop-up message box

3 Tips To Master QTP/UFT Within 30 Days
http://tinyurl.com/3-Tips-For-QTP-UFT

Free Webinars, Videos, and Live Trainings
http://tinyurl.com/Free-QTP-UFT-Selenium

SecondsToWait	Value specifying the maximum number of seconds to display the pop-up message box
Title	Value specifying the text that will appear as the pop-up message title
Type	Value specifying the type of buttons and icons that will appear in the message box
Button	Value specifying the number of the button that will be clicked to dismiss the message box

Quit Method

The Quit method forces the current script to stop and return the specified error code. The following is the syntax for Quit method:

Syntax
Object.Quit (ReturnExitCode)

Figure 7.91 – Quit Method Syntax Details

Argument	Description
Object	Name of a WScript object
ReturnExitCode	Code value returned by the program after exiting

Read Method

The Read method returns a specified number of characters from an input stream. The following is the syntax for Read method:

Syntax
Object.Read (Characters)

Figure 7.92 – Read Method Syntax Details

Argument	Description
Object	StdIn text stream object

Characters	Value specifying the number of characters that will be read

Note: The StdIn, StdOut, and StdErr properties and methods work when accessed while utilizing CScript. However, an error occurs if accessed by WScript.

ReadAll Method

The ReadAll method returns all characters from an input stream. The following is the syntax for ReadAll method:

Syntax
Object.ReadAll

Figure 7.93 – ReadAll Method Syntax Details

Argument	**Description**
Object	StdIn text stream object

Note: The StdIn, StdOut, and StdErr properties and methods work when accessed while utilizing CScript. However, an error occurs if accessed by WScript.

ReadLine Method

The ReadLine method returns an entire line from an input stream. The following is the syntax for ReadLine method:

Syntax
Object.ReadLine

Figure 7.94 – ReadLine Method Syntax Details

Argument	**Description**
Object	Name of a WshShell object

3 Tips To Master QTP/UFT Within 30 Days
http://tinyurl.com/3-Tips-For-QTP-UFT

Free Webinars, Videos, and Live Trainings
http://tinyurl.com/Free-QTP-UFT-Selenium

Note: The StdIn, StdOut, and StdErr properties and methods work when accessed while utilizing CScript. However, an error occurs if accessed by WScript.

RegDelete Method

The RegDelete method removes a key or one of its values from the registry. The following is the syntax for RegDelete method:

Syntax
Object.RegDelete (Name)

Figure 7.95 – RegDelete Method Syntax Details

Argument	Description
Object	Name of a WshShell object
Name	Value specifying the name of the registry key or key value that will be deleted

A key name is specified by ending the Name with a backslash while the value name is specified by leaving off the backslash. The following is five root key names and abbreviations:

Figure 7.96 – Root Key Names and Abbreviations

Root Key Name	Abbreviation
HKEY_CURRENT_USER	HKCU
HKEY_LOCAL_MACHINE	HKLM
HKEY_CLASSES_ROOT	HKCR
HKEY_USERS	HKEY_USERS
HKEY_CURRENT_CONFIG	HKEY_CURRENT_CONFIG

RegRead Method

The RegRead method reads and returns the value of a key or value name from the registry. The following is the syntax for RegRead method:

Skype: rex.jones34
Twitter: @RexJonesII
Email: Rex.Jones@Test4Success.org
LinkedIn: https://www.linkedin.com/in/rexjones34

Syntax
Object.RegRead (Name)

Figure 7.97 – RegRead Method Syntax Details

Argument	Description
Object	Name of a WshShell object
Name	Value specifying the key or value name

The following five values are returned for RegRead method:

Figure 7.98 – Values Returned for RegRead Method

Type	Description
REG_SZ	A string
REG_DWORD	A number
REG_BINARY	A binary value
REG_EXPAND_SZ	An expandable string
REG_MULTI_SZ	An array of string

A key name is specified by ending the Name with a backslash while the value name is specified by leaving off the backslash. The value entry has three elements (name, data type, and value). To read a key's default value, the name of the key must be specified. Full key names and value names begin with a root key. The following is five root key names and abbreviations:

Figure 7.99 – Root Key Names and Abbreviations

Root Key Name	Abbreviation
HKEY_CURRENT_USER	HKCU
HKEY_LOCAL_MACHINE	HKLM
HKEY_CLASSES_ROOT	HKCR
HKEY_USERS	HKEY_USERS

3 Tips To Master QTP/UFT Within 30 Days
http://tinyurl.com/3-Tips-For-QTP-UFT

Free Webinars, Videos, and Live Trainings
http://tinyurl.com/Free-QTP-UFT-Selenium

HKEY_CURRENT_CONFIG	HKEY_CURRENT_CONFIG

RegWrite Method
The RegWrite method writes an entry into the registry. This method creates a new key, add a value name to an existing key, or changes the value of an existing value name. The following is the syntax for RegWrite method:

Syntax
Object.RegWrite (Name, Value [, Type])

Figure 7.100 – RegWrite Method Syntax Details

Argument	Description
Object	Name of a WshShell object
Name	Value specifying key name, value name, or value to create, add, or change
Value	Name of the new key that will be created, name of the value that will be added to an existing key, or new value to assign to an existing value name
Type	Value specifying the value's data type

Full key names and value names are prefixed with a root key. The following is five root key names and abbreviations:

Figure 7.101 – Root Key Names and Abbreviations

Root Key Name	Abbreviation
HKEY_CURRENT_USER	HKCU
HKEY_LOCAL_MACHINE	HKLM
HKEY_CLASSES_ROOT	HKCR
HKEY_USERS	HKEY_USERS
HKEY_CURRENT_CONFIG	HKEY_CURRENT_CONFIG

The following is four data types that can be specified with the argument Type:

Figure 7.102 – Data Types

Converted to	Type
String	REG_SZ
String	REG_EXPAND_SZ
Integer	REG_DWORD
Integer	REG_BINARY

Remove Method

The Remove method deletes an existing environment variable with a specified name. The following is the syntax for Remove method:

Syntax
Object.Remove (Name)

Figure 7.103 – Remove Method Syntax Details

Argument	Description
Object	Name of a WshEnvironment object
Name	Value specifying the environment variable name that will be deleted

RemoveNetworkDrive Method

The RemoveNetworkDrive method removes a previously shared network drive from the computer system. The following is the syntax for RemoveNetworkDrive method:

Syntax
Object.RemoveNetworkDrive (Name, [Force], [UpdateProfile])

Figure 7.104 – RemoveNetworkDrive Method Syntax Details

Argument	Description

Object	Name of a WshNetwork object
Name	Value specifying the mapped drive name (local or remote name) that will be removed
Force	Value specifying if a removal of the mapped drive is forced. True indicates the connections are removed
UpdateProfile	Boolean value specifying if the mapping from a user's profile is removed. True: Mapping is removed from the user's profile False: (Default) Mapping is not removed from the user's profile

RemovePrinterConnection Method

The RemovePrinterConnection method removes a previously shared network printer connection from the computer system. The following is the syntax for RemovePrinterConnection method:

Syntax
Object.RemovePrinterConnection (Name, [Force], [UpdateProfile])

Figure 7.105 – RemovePrinterConnection Method Syntax Details

Argument	Description
Object	Name of a WshNetwork object
Name	Value specifying the name that identifies the printer
Force	Boolean value specifying if a removal of the mapped printer is removed. True indicates the printer connection is removed
UpdateProfile	Boolean value specifying if a change in the user's profile is saved. True: Change in the user's profile is saved False: (Default) Change in the user's profile is not saved

Run Method

The Run method runs an application (program) in a new process. The following is the syntax for Run method:

Skype: rex.jones34
Twitter: @RexJonesII
Email: Rex.Jones@Test4Success.org
LinkedIn: https://www.linkedin.com/in/rexjones34

Syntax

Object.Run (Command, [WindowStyle], [WaitOnReturn])

Figure 7.106 – Run Method Syntax Details

Argument	Description
Object	Name of a WshShell object
Command	Value specifying the command line
WindowStyle	Value specifying the appearance of the program's window
WaitOnReturn	Boolean value specifying if the script will wait for the program to finish executing before continuing to the next statement: True: Script execution stops until the program finishes while Run returns an error code returned by the program False: (Default) Run method returns immediately after starting the program

The following are settings for the WindowStyle argument:

Figure 7.107 – WindowStyle Settings

WindowStyle	Settings
0	Hides the window and activates another window
1	Activates and displays a window
2	Activates the window and displays it as a minimized window
3	Activates the window and displays it as a maximized window
4	Displays a window in its most recent size and position
5	Activates the window and displays it in its current size and position
6	Minimizes the specified window and activates the next top-level window in the Z order
7	Displays the window as a minimized window
8	Displays the window in its current state
9	Activates and displays the window
10	Sets the show state based on the state of the program that started the application

3 Tips To Master QTP/UFT Within 30 Days
http://tinyurl.com/3-Tips-For-QTP-UFT

Free Webinars, Videos, and Live Trainings
http://tinyurl.com/Free-QTP-UFT-Selenium

Save Method

The Save method saves the shortcut at a specified location. Each location is specified by the FullName property. The following is the syntax for Save method:

Syntax
Object.Save

Figure 7.108 – Save Method Syntax Details

Argument	Description
Object	Name of a WshShortcut or WshURLShortcut object

SendKeys Method

The SendKeys method sends one or more keystrokes to the active window. The following is the syntax for SendKeys method:

Syntax
Object.SendKeys (KeyStroke)

Figure 7.109 – SendKeys Method Syntax Details

Argument	Description
Object	Name of a WshShell object
KeyStroke	Value specifying the keystroke or keystrokes that will be sent

SetDefaultPrinter Method

The SetDefaultPrinter method sets the default printer to the specified remote printer. The following is the syntax for SetDefaultPrinter method:

Syntax
Object.SetDefaultPrinter (PrinterName)

Skype: rex.jones34
Twitter: @RexJonesII
Email: Rex.Jones@Test4Success.org
LinkedIn: https://www.linkedin.com/in/rexjones34

Figure 7.110 – SetDefaultPrinter Method Syntax Details

Argument	Description
Object	Name of a WshNetwork object
PrinterName	Value specifying the remote printer's Universal Naming Convention (UNC) name

ShowUsage Method

The ShowUsage method produces a self-documenting script by showing information about how the script should be used. The following is the syntax for ShowUsage method:

Syntax

Object.ShowUsage

Figure 7.111 – ShowUsage Method Syntax Details

Argument	Description
Object	Name of a WScript object

Sign Method

The Sign method signs a script stored in a string. The following is the syntax for Sign method:

Syntax

Object.Sign (FileExtension, Text, Certificate, Store)

Figure 7.112 – Sign Method Syntax Details

Argument	Description
Object	Scripting.Signer
FileExtension	A string designating the script extension type (.vbs, .js, or .wsf). This provides a mechanism by which the operating system can determine the type of script file being verified

3 Tips To Master QTP/UFT Within 30 Days
http://tinyurl.com/3-Tips-For-QTP-UFT

Free Webinars, Videos, and Live Trainings
http://tinyurl.com/Free-QTP-UFT-Selenium

Text	A string containing the script to be signed
Certificate	A string designating the author's certificate name
Store	A string designating the name of the certificate store

SignFile Method

The SignFile method signs a script using a digital signature. The following is the syntax for SignFile method:

Syntax
Object.SignFile (FileName, Certificate, Store)

Figure 7.113 – SignFile Method Syntax Details

Argument	Description
Object	Scripting.Signer
FileName	A string containing the script file name
Certificate	A string designating the author's certificate name
Store	A string designating the name of the certificate store

Skip Method

The Skip method skips a specified number of characters when reading from an input text stream. The following is the syntax for Skip method:

Syntax
Object.Skip (Characters)

Figure 7.114 – Skip Method Syntax Details

Argument	Description
Object	StdIn text stream object
Characters	Value specifying the number of characters that will be skipped

Note: The StdIn, StdOut, and StdErr properties and methods work when accessed while utilizing CScript. However, an error occurs if accessed by WScript.

SkipLine Method

The SkipLine method skips the next line when reading from an input stream. The following is the syntax for SkipLine method:

Syntax
Object.SkipLine

Figure 7.115 – SkipLine Method Syntax Details

Argument	Description
Object	StdIn text stream object

Note: The StdIn, StdOut, and StdErr properties and methods work when accessed while utilizing CScript. However, an error occurs if accessed by WScript.

Sleep Method

The Sleep method forces execution of the current script to be inactive for a specified length of time then continue execution of the script. The following is the syntax for Sleep method:

Syntax
Object.Sleep (Time)

Figure 7.116 – Sleep Method Syntax Details

Argument	Description
Object	Name of a WScript object
Time	Value in milliseconds to suspend the current script execution

Terminate Method (WshScriptExec)

The Terminate method (WshScriptExec) directs the script engine to end the process initiated by the Exec method. The following is the syntax for Terminate method (WshScriptExec):

Syntax
Object.Terminate

Figure 7.117 – Terminate Method (WshScriptExec) Syntax Details

Argument	Description
Object	Name of a WshScriptExec object

Verify Method

The Verify method verifies a digital signature retrieved as a string. The following is the syntax for Verify method:

Syntax
Object.Verify (FileExtension, Text, ShowUI)

Figure 7.118 – Verify Method Syntax Details

Argument	Description
Object	Scripting.Signer
FileExtension	A string designating the script extension type (.vbs, .js, or .wsf). This provides a mechanism by which the operating system can determine the type of script file being verified
Text	Text that will be verified
ShowUI	Boolean value (True or False) True: The Scripting.Signer object may create dialog boxes to prompt the user if there is not sufficient information to determine trust False: The Scripting.Signer object determines if a trusted source provided the signature without prompting the user

Chapter 7
Windows Script Host (WSH)   You Must Learn VBScript for QTP/UFT

VerifyFile Method

The VerifyFile method verifies the digital signature encapsulated in a script. The following is the syntax for VerifyFile method:

Syntax
Object.VerifyFile (FileName, ShowUI)

Figure 7.119 – VerifyFile Method Syntax Details

Argument	Description
Object	Scripting.Signer
FileName	A string containing the script file name
ShowUI	Boolean value (True or False) True: The Scripting.Signer object may create dialog boxes to prompt the user if there is not sufficient information to determine trust False: The Scripting.Signer object determines if a trusted source provided the signature without prompting the user

Write Method

The Write method sends a string to an output stream. The following is the syntax for Write method:

Syntax
Object.Write (Text)

Figure 7.120 – Write Method Syntax Details

Argument	Description
Object	StdOut or StdErr text stream objects
Text	Value specifying the text that will be written to the stream

3 Tips To Master QTP/UFT Within 30 Days
http://tinyurl.com/3-Tips-For-QTP-UFT

Free Webinars, Videos, and Live Trainings
http://tinyurl.com/Free-QTP-UFT-Selenium

Note: The StdIn, StdOut, and StdErr properties and methods work when accessed while utilizing CScript. However, an error occurs if accessed by WScript.

WriteBlankLines Method

The WriteBlankLines method sends a specified number of blank lines to an output stream. The following is the syntax for WriteBlankLines method:

Syntax
Object.WriteBlankLines (Lines)

Figure 7.121 – WriteBlankLines Method Syntax Details

Argument	Description
Object	StdOut or StdErr text stream objects
Lines	Value specifying the number of blank lines that will be written to the stream

Note: The StdIn, StdOut, and StdErr properties and methods work when accessed while utilizing CScript. However, an error occurs if accessed by WScript.

WriteLine Method

The WriteLine method sends a string with a newline character to an output stream. The following is the syntax for WriteLine method:

Syntax
Object.WriteLine (Text)

Figure 7.122 – WriteLine Method Syntax Details

Argument	Description
Object	StdOut or StdErr text stream objects
Text	Value specifying the text that will be written to the stream. A newline character is written to the output stream if the value is omitted

Chapter 7
Windows Script Host (WSH)   You Must Learn VBScript for QTP/UFT

Note: The StdIn, StdOut, and StdErr properties and methods work when accessed while utilizing CScript. However, an error occurs if accessed by WScript.

Chapter 7 provides information regarding Windows Script Host (WSH) which is an administration tool for Windows. There are 14 objects in the WSH Object model, along with several methods and properties. Chapter 8 will discuss Windows Management Instrumentation (WMI). WMI manages hardware and software in a Windows based environment.

Chapter 8
Windows Management
Instrumentation (WMI)

Windows Management Instrumentation (WMI) is a collection of tools within the Windows driver model that permits VBScript to manage PC's and servers. The PC's and servers can be connected locally or remotely. In a nutshell, WMI is utilized to manage hardware and software in a Windows based environment.

However, WMI must be in accordance with the standards established by the Distributed Management Task Force (DMTF). The DMTF is an organization that works with technology vendors to describe interoperable management solutions. This organization facilitates WMI to manage distributed enterprise systems for servers and workstations powered by the Windows Operating Systems (OS).

Chapter 8 will cover the following regarding WMI:

- ✓ WMI Architecture Layers
- ✓ WMI Operating System Classes

WMI Architecture Layers

The WMI architectural layers are fundamentals underlying the design of hardware and software. These layers help build WMI which is an industry initiative to expand a standard technology for accessing management information. The following is a list of three WMI Architecture Layers:

- o Managed Resources

Skype: rex.jones34
Twitter: @RexJonesII
Email: Rex.Jones@Test4Success.org
LinkedIn: https://www.linkedin.com/in/rexjones34

- o WMI Infrastructure
- o Consumers

Managed Resources

The Managed Resources layer includes devices, services, or any other entity that grants information through a provider. The provider is a layer between the managed resources and their native interfaces to the Common Information Model (CIM). Information is made available in the form of classes, methods, and attributes.

WMI Infrastructure

The WMI Infrastructure layer is a component that receive calls from consumers delivered to the managed devices or elements. Common Information Model Object Manager (CIMOM) is a primary component in the WMI Infrastructure. CIMOM manages CIM objects (i.e., printer, disk drive, etc.) on a Web Based Enterprise Management (WBEM) enabled system. In addition, CIMOM assist in delivering connectivity between the clients and devices.

Consumers

The Consumers layer utilizes the exposed classes and completes the job. Jobs can include scripts and executables written in VBScript. This helps query WMI classes and receive specific information regarding a device.

WMI Operating System Classes

The WMI Operating System classes is a category that gathers classes serving as operating system related objects. They represent different kinds of configurations and settings that define a computing environment. There are many WMI Operating System classes which grant an opportunity to retrieve information. However, the following is a list of some Win32 WMI Operating System classes:

3 Tips To Master QTP/UFT Within 30 Days
http://tinyurl.com/3-Tips-For-QTP-UFT

Free Webinars, Videos, and Live Trainings
http://tinyurl.com/Free-QTP-UFT-Selenium

Chapter 8
Windows Management
Instrumentation (WMI)   You Must Learn VBScript for QTP/UFT

Figure 8.1 – Win32 WMI Operating System Classes

Win32_ComputerSystem	Win32_Registry
Win32_Desktop	Win32_ScheduledJob
Win32_Environment	Win32_Service
Win32_Group	Win32_Share
Win32_OperatingSystem	Win32_ShortcutFile
Win32_Process	Win32_Timezone

Win32_ComputerSystem
The Win32_ComputerSystem is a WMI class serving as a computer system running Windows.

Win32_Desktop
The Win32_Desktop is a WMI class serving as the common characteristics of a user's desktop. This class has properties that can be modified by the user to customize the desktop.

Win32_Environment
The Win32_Environment is a WMI class serving as an environment or system environment setting on a Windows computer system.

Win32_Group
The Win32_Group is a WMI class serving as data about a group account. A group account allows access privileges to be changed for a list of users.

Win32_OperatingSystem
The Win32_OperatingSystem is a WMI class serving as a Windows based operating system installed on a computer.

Win32_Process
The Win32_Process is a WMI class serving as a process on an operating system.

Skype: rex.jones34
Twitter: @RexJonesII
Email: Rex.Jones@Test4Success.org
LinkedIn: https://www.linkedin.com/in/rexjones34

Chapter 8
Windows Management
Instrumentation (WMI)   You Must Learn VBScript for QTP/UFT

Win32_Registry
The Win32_Registry is a WMI class serving as the system registry on a computer system running Windows.

Win32_ScheduledJob
The Win32_ScheduledJob is a WMI class serving as a job created with the AT command.

Win32_Service
The Win32_Service is a WMI class serving as a service on a computer system running Windows.

Win32_Share
The Win32_Share is a WMI class serving as a shared resource on a computer system running Windows.

Win32_ShortcutFile
The Win32_ShortcutFile is a WMI class serving as files that are shortcuts to other files, directories, and commands.

Win32_Timezone
The Win32_Timezone is a WMI class serving as the time zone information for a computer system running Windows, which includes the changes required for transitioning to the daylight saving time.

3 Tips To Master QTP/UFT Within 30 Days
http://tinyurl.com/3-Tips-For-QTP-UFT

Free Webinars, Videos, and Live Trainings
http://tinyurl.com/Free-QTP-UFT-Selenium

Conclusion

Part 2—You Must Learn VBScript for QTP/UFT targeted the deeper concepts of VBScript. VBScript is a lightweight scripting language that has powerful features which supports QTP/UFT scripts. As a result, the powerful features enable scripts to be written with less lines of code. The following are topics from this book:

<u>Dictionary Objects</u>: Dictionary Objects consist of all kinds of data such as, strings, dates, arrays, and other objects. The data is stored in key/item pairs as an associative array.

<u>FileSystemObject (FSO)</u>: FSO allows files, folders, and drives associated to the computer system to be created, read, or located.

<u>Classes</u>: Classes are containers for objects where an object can store data via properties and perform an action via methods.

<u>Regular Expressions</u>: Regular expressions are tools for searching and replacing data. The RegExp object is a built-in object which provides regular expressions.

<u>Debugging and Handling Errors</u>: Debugging is the process of locating and fixing errors while handling errors anticipates, detects, and resolves errors.

<u>Windows Script Host (WSH)</u>: Windows Script Host (WSH) is an administration tool that establishes an environment for hosting scripts.

<u>Windows Management Instrumentation (WMI)</u>: Windows Management Instrumentation (WMI) is a collection of tools that allows VBScript to manage PCs and servers.

Skype: rex.jones34
Twitter: @RexJonesII
Email: Rex.Jones@Test4Success.org
LinkedIn: https://www.linkedin.com/in/rexjones34

Download PDF Version

The PDF Version of this book is available to you at the following link.

http://tinyurl.com/VBScript-4-QTP-UFT-Part-2

If the book was helpful, can you leave a favorable review?

http://tinyurl.com/Review-Part-2-VBScript-4-QTP

Thanks in advance,

Rex Allen Jones II

3 Tips To Master QTP/UFT Within 30 Days
http://tinyurl.com/3-Tips-For-QTP-UFT

Free Webinars, Videos, and Live Trainings
http://tinyurl.com/Free-QTP-UFT-Selenium

Books by Rex Jones II

1. **Free Book** Absolute Beginner
   (Part 1) You Must Learn VBScript for QTP/UFT
   Don't Ignore The Language For Functional Automation Testing

2. (Part 2) You Must Learn VBScript for QTP/UFT
   Don't Ignore The Language For Functional Automation Testing

3. **Free Book** Absolute Beginner
   (Part 1) Java 4 Selenium WebDriver
   Come Learn How To Program For Automation Testing

4. (Part 2) Java 4 Selenium WebDriver
   Come Learn How To Program For Automation Testing

Coming Soon

5. **Free Book** Absolute Beginner
   (Part 1) Selenium WebDriver for Functional Automation Testing
   Your Beginners Guide To Become Good

6. (Part 2) Selenium WebDriver for Functional Automation Testing
   Your Guide To Stay Effective

Skype: rex.jones34
Twitter: @RexJonesII
Email: Rex.Jones@Test4Success.org
LinkedIn: https://www.linkedin.com/in/rexjones34

3 Tips To Master QTP/UFT Within 30 Days
http://tinyurl.com/3-Tips-For-QTP-UFT

Free Webinars, Videos, and Live Trainings
http://tinyurl.com/Free-QTP-UFT-Selenium

Sign Up To Receive

1. 3 Tips To Master QTP/UFT Within 30 Days
   http://tinyurl.com/3-Tips-For-QTP-UFT

2. 3 Tips To Master Selenium Within 30 Days
   http://tinyurl.com/3-Tips-For-Selenium

3. Free Webinars, Videos, and Live Trainings
   http://tinyurl.com/Free-QTP-UFT-Selenium

Skype: rex.jones34
Twitter: @RexJonesII
Email: Rex.Jones@Test4Success.org
LinkedIn: https://www.linkedin.com/in/rexjones34

Made in the USA
Las Vegas, NV
17 April 2022

47605289R00162